How To Make

EASY MONEY
IN
ANTIQUES

Without Even Half-Way Trying

by

DAN SHIARAS

in collaboration with
and illustrated by
Fran Swarbrick

COLLECTOR BOOKS
A Division of Schroeder Publishing Co., Inc.
P.O. Box 3009 ● PADUCAH, KENTUCKY ● 42001

The current values in this book should be used only as a guide. They are not intended to set prices, which vary from one section of the country to another. Auction prices as well as dealer prices vary greatly and are affected by condition as well as demand. Neither the Author nor the Publisher assumes responsibility for any losses that might be incurred as a result of consulting this guide.

All the incidents related in this book are true, but some names have been changed.

TABLE OF CONTENTS

1

TOP-SECRET INFORMATION THAT CAN MAKE YOU THOUSANDS EACH YEAR

The first thing to do if you want to make money with antiques is to buy a current *Schroeder's Antiques Price Guide*. Study it until you know it well, and carry it with you. Then start visiting antique shops each day as much as time allows. If you don't already have a favorite antique, see what speaks to you, and pick two or three to concentrate on.

With each visit to a shop, ask a question or two about your favorite collectible. Most shops will let you handle the items you are interested in at your own risk. You must pick up an antique dish or bank to get the feel of it. It is the only way to learn the difference between the old and the new, and after two years of constantly looking and handling, you will know the difference.

In the meantime, you should attend auctions when

possible. An aspiring dealer can reach perfection only by going to all the good and bad sales he can possibly attend to watch what antiques are selling for. He must file in his mind all he has seen, so that at some other sale where bidders are not knowledgeable, he can step in and buy his first antique bargain.

So you must keep working at the antique craft, just as a great musician practices each day.

But do not spend all your time or a lot of money at auction sales. The big money is not where the competition is harder to penetrate than the Maginot Line. It is useless to run all over to auction sales, garage sales, or rummage sales on the chance that the illusive $100,000 signed Tiffany lamp will be there for $100. With everyone in a family all geared up to grab Aunt Anna's covered-wagon-era antiques when she departs this life, your chances are not good nowadays to buy even one antique reasonably at auction sales.

What I am going to tell you now is either going to make or break you in seriously becoming a top-flight, money-making dealer. Pull out a map of your area and draw a ring with a 75-mile radius around your town. Note the towns in your circle which you feel might have good antiques.

By this time you have decided which antiques you would like to specialize in, perhaps only one. Now place ads in area newspapers stating what you will pay for your specialties. Then sit back and let your ads work for you, which they will do day and night. Sometimes just when you feel you have fed the "ad kitty" long enough, you will hit the jackpot.

I know how it feels to receive a call from a nearby town about an oriental rug, and see a great, 24-foot mint Kerman on the floor. One day in 1974 my wife,

Fran, and I drove to Rockford to buy an oriental rug, and ended up buying a U-Haul trailer full of mint Sarouks, Kermans, and Chinese carpets. The profit from this one lick alone paid for all the advertising I would do in that town for 500 years.

This has worked for me, and it will work for you. No matter what you advertise to buy, the items will come out of their elusive hiding places to be bought by you.

In past years, I bagged close to 1,000 Indian rugs through local and national ads, and for ten years led the nation in buying and selling Mettlach steins and Royal Doulton figurines and tobies. I sure didn't do this by checking out the local garage and rummage sales. I did it by placing wanted-to-buy ads in all the big national trade papers, and then I watched all I advertised for come rolling in.

This success in advertising made me serious about becoming a millionaire. I felt that if the great art objects of the country would keep flooding in, I could soon quit this hard business and go sailing on my private yacht in the Gulf of Mexico. My dreams did almost come true for me. I quit because I had lost the drive to make big money after I had reached only a few of my goals, such as owning the most beautiful home in the Cape Cod class in America, and driving an expensive new car every year.

I am passing these hints along to you so you can begin to live the good life that I have been leading. To begin with, while letting your ads sniff out bargains for you, you should stay with what you do for a living. Let your antique-buying be just a side-line until you have tried it for three or four years.

If you are determined to go to garage sales, pick out

the ones in rich neighborhoods. Since I promised to give you top secret information, I will reveal some ruses of dealers. To gain the jump on competitors, they will go to the newspaper office when the paper is about to be issued and get a copy, then scan the garage sales for the best prospects and drive there a day early. If they have a convincing enough story about why they can't come the next day, they may make some good money by "creaming" the goodies.

Another ploy of dealers is to drive around in area towns and spot lace curtains in an old house, often a sign of old people living in it. On the pretense of using their phone for an emergency call, the dealer will give the house's contents the once-over. It's a 50-50 chance that when he gets in the door of a loaded house, he will buy. Imagine a signed Goddard 1780-90 Chippendale sideboard for $1,000 that will be worth $250,000 to $300,000 at Eastern auctions!

Such a windfall came my way in 1968, but at an auction. I bought a Rockford barber's inlaid eagles Hepplewhite sideboard at his auction for $300, and sold it for $800 the next day, only to learn it was worth $30,000. It was a case of doing everything right that I'd learned in buying, but fouling out in selling.

Here are some of my best money-makers in the antique-buying line. You will hear more about many of them later in this book, as I try to impress you indelibly with what to keep your eyes open for. Be alert for old magazines whenever you go into an attic or basement. Watch for pre-1940 copies of **_Ladies' Home Journal, Woman's Home Companion, Saturday Evening Post, Vanity Fair, Delineator, Vogue, Theatre, McCall's, Pictorial Review._** They are often worth their weight in gold. Don't stop bidding at a sale until they are yours. All are loaded with items of value. **Pictorial Review** has the famous, high-priced Dolly Dingle cut-outs. **Ladies' Home Journal** contains both Betty Bonnet 1911-1920 doll cut-outs as well as the 1924-1928 Kewpie pages by Rose O'Neill, all worth over $10 a page.

   Saturday Evening Post has $10 Norman Rockwell covers. **Delineators** are loaded with fashions, and **Theatre** magazines that I used to sell for $7 a copy are now selling for double. Be on the look-out for old five-cent 1930's pulps like **Shadow, Spider, G-8, Phantom,** and hundreds more. If they say five cents on the cover, do not stop bidding short of a stroke or a coronary, because the great, rare pulps sometimes sell for $100 each. It is nothing to sell a five-cent **Shadow** pulp for $200, and you will be thanked for selling it. I call items such as these "sleepers".

   Other magazines that are worth a bundle are 1895-1939 steel-wheel tractor magazines, along with farm machinery catalogues, mainly the Case and Rumley steam engine catalogs. The Waterloo Boy, Hart-Paar, Pausen, Case, and Rumley Steam Engine catalogues sell for $100 up, so if you buy a hundred of them out of some attic, a $10,000 check may be yours from the collectors I know.

   Classic car catalogues in color from the 1920's and 1930's are selling for $50 apiece and more nowadays. A car showroom brochure in color is better three-to-one than black and white. I sold a ton of these beautiful catalogs in the 1960's, but then they all but disappeared. Every once in a while I pick one up at a house I go on call to, and I cash it in for about $50 to an Eastern collector.

   Fishing tackle is another big money-maker today.

Who would ever guess that an old wooden lure, even with fine, original paint and glass eyes, is worth up to $150? The average 1920's glass-eyed lure retails for $10. The one thing to look for is glass eyes and not painted eyes. Most painted-eye lures are not wood but early 1940's plastic. Lures are a sleeper paying good dividends for me.

Whoever heard of an old 1920's wooden-handled ice cream scoop selling for $75? I just sold a rare sandwich-maker scoop for $60, also a cone-shaped scoop for the same amount.

The sleepers I have named can fit in with your specialities. I mention them to point out that is is not the things that everyone knows are worth big profits that can help you become successful, but often the ones that less than 5% know about, in the gray areas of antique collecting.

By this time you need to have a ready market available for your big pile of antiques. No. 1 in doing this is to subscribe to the most-read trade paper, the **Antique Trader** weekly, Dubuque, Iowa. Religiously scan the entire paper every week. Read the "Antiques Wanted" section over, and then read it over and over again until you have almost memorized it. Nearly all the big dealers and collectors in America have advertised in the classified section of this newspaper at some time.

I will go right down the "Miscellaneous Wanted" ads in the **Trader** and list all the items that have made me big money by advertising for them in local or national papers. Nippon is No. 1. Another is old gasoline pump advertising globes that once sat on the top of nine-foot hand-operated pumps. Some, like Eagle gasoline globes, retail for $2,500 each, while Sinclair

Aircraft gasoline globes sell for $600. An ad for gasoline globes usually will kick out not only one or two globes, but the old gas pumps, which sell for around $400. They are often lying around in farmers' barns and are not wanted, so you can sometimes buy them quite reasonably.

Old candy store 13-inch-wide brass National Cash Registers sell for $600 easily to dealers. Anything railroad is a big seller, with white brakemen's lanterns retailing for $40, red for $60. Blue glass hand lanterns are $100. At a just-concluded auction I saw a green lantern globe alone with CB&Q on it sell for a record $750. It was a very rare lantern color and an even rarer price. Railroad china sells for an easy $100 per piece, up to $200 each for a Santa Fe Railroad china dish.

Old-time padlocks bring good prices. A stock-ticker and its old-time glass globe means an automatic $600 up for you. Big old swirled marbles are worth $50 in the two-inch sizes, less for the smaller ones.

Remember, you don't have to worry about selling these sleepers, because you can write to their advertisers in the *Trader* for instant cash.

Pre-1940 Erector sets easily fetch you $60, and they show up many times at big antique sales or in dusty house attics where your ads will take you oftener than you think possible.

Quilts have been big, big money-makers over the past 30 years for me. Buy only the quilts that are pre-1940 and hand-made. Don't buy a spotted or torn quilt. A blue decor quilt will outsell all others three to one, with red second. Try to stay under $100 in the Midwest whenever you buy a quilt for resale at $150. For antique applique quilts you can pay $200 and sell for $300 to $500 by sending a photo to quilt buyers.

Watch for antique brass microscopes, which easily sell for $1,000, while the black metal ones bring about $100. Old surgical and dental instruments sell for almost their weight in gold. Wood-handled instruments are the highest priced, then come black-handled ones, which are followed by the steel-handled. A small box of any of these brings from $500 to $10,000 for the wood-handled type. An 1800 dental instrument called a turnkey sells for $150 if all metal and $400 if made of ivory. Not too far back I bought three turnkeys for $13 at a local auction and sold them to a dental museum in Alabama for $375. You can do the same sort of thing by working hard to teach yourself about the most-wanted collectibles.

Old paintings are valuable if they are the right signed ones. A friend of mine went to a sale with me in Rockford a few years ago and made the purchase of his life when he picked up two signed Kruseman (19th Century Flemish artist) works called "Summer" and "Winter" for $105 each. He took them to the Sotheby Parke Bernet Galleries in New York city, where they sold at $14,500 for "Summer" and $18,500 for "Winter". That day in Rockford they leaned against a tree in the rain. Luckily the auctioneer had put a plastic cover over them.

This shows you that the big money is still out there. The previous year at another Rockford auction, one of the 20 best Tiffany lamps ever made turned up. As detailed in another story, it was mistakenly called an old "metal" lamp by the owner as she made out her own sale bill because she did not want auctioneers in her house. The lamp sold for $13,500. Shortly after, an exact mate to this lamp sold at Sotheby's New York auction gallery for $85,000.

Back to the sleepers--odd-shaped typewriters may sell for $1,000. Most of the strange-looking old typewriters retail for $300 to $500 and may find a market, with all the rest I have mentioned, with those who advertise in the *Trader*.

I am currently advertising to buy one of the biggest money-making sleepers of all my years in the antique business. My ad reads that I want to buy the beautiful art works forgotten so long which are signed Nippon--vases, plates, plaques, tobacco humidors, chocolate sets, etc. In Nippon, stay with the richly hand-painted pieces. The vase that is encrusted with much gold and roses is worth ten times more than one with only gold tracery on white.

This exciting Nippon field was just this year opened to me by accident. I ran a large ad in the *Trader* one day in 1982 to sell around 100 different antiques, with a few of them pictured. One of them was a rose-decorated cracker jar in Nippon. My phone did not stop ringing the whole week that the ad came out. Up until this time I had never bid on Nippon, putting it in the same class as other early 20th Century Japanese objects. I soon found out that the Nippon pieces that are made with the main decorative scheme in relief ("blow-outs") can be worth from $600-$1,500.

I think the best antique for you to concentrate on first with your ads is Nippon, advertising for "Nippon wanted." Nippon is a sure-fire way to make money in the antique business without half trying. All you have to do is make an all-out effort to buy it. It is easy to recognize because it is signed "hand-painted Nippon" on the bottom. This is probably the last year or two for Nippon to be sold cheaply at sales.

Here are some sample Nippon prices: a tobacco

humidor with gold and roses can be sold for $400, while one with dogs' heads in relief or standing away from the rest of the piece will bring $600 or $700. Just

Molded in relief Nippon humidor $850-$1,000; Nippon plaque, $300-$400.

the past month I purchased a 12-inch camel and driver blow-out along with a 4″ dog blow-out tobacco humidor for $320, worth $1,200.

Stay with Nippon. It is plentiful as of this writing, but nearly worth its weight in gold.

An advantage I have had in the antique business is my experience, beginning as a stamp and coin collector at eight years of age. Later I was an antique dealer half of the time, and a horse, cow, sheep, pig, and billy goat dealer the rest of the time. I was known for 22 years as Old No. 40, the shiftiest livestock dealer in all of Illinois. I would buy 200 head of feeder pigs or cattle with one wink of the eye, and this bidding experience came in handy later at antique auctions.

I get myself psyched up to buy at a great antique auction a couple of days ahead of time, when I read the auctioneer's sale bill. If I read of several Navajo rugs or Mettlach steins, I have bought them as soon as I read about them, and if anybody dares cross my bidding path the day of the auction, they will soon find out it would have been better to move to another sale.

I have a big advantage over many others who buy at auctions, in that I have a photographic memory that allows me to store up all the prices I have sold for, plus all the prices of items I have lost to other buyers.

"Buy low, sell high" is the lullaby my Greek mother used to rock me to sleep with. Now I am sharing with you some of the secrets I have learned along the way. When you are out buying in person, never make an offer on anything unless you are going to be forced to leave without it. People usually know what they want for their things. If you have to make an offer and offer high, the seller will begin to think the items are very valuable, and it will cause a big research project to get underway as to what the articles are really worth. The less you say, the better, when you are out buying.

I will have to be honest with you and tell you that, unfortunately, hanging the name "antique dealer" on a person seems to give him the license to steal antiques legally by paying near-zero prices for them. As far back as I can remember, I knew dealers who would go into a home, and if an old couple had antiques to sell, not knowing what their fine things were worth, the dealer would give them such a low price it was just the same as stealing. Stealing from widows and orphans is not commendable, but it is the route that 90% of the dealers I knew were taking in the 1960's and are still taking. Just one good thing can be said-- if they "Jesse Jamesed" a person, they would never show the antiques they bought so cheaply at an area antique show, since they would not want the "pigeon" to see what a huge mark-up was put on the antique. I know for certain if I have purchased a Sarouk throw rug for $300 and I have $3,500 on it in my antique booth, the seller might call the cops, and I wouldn't blame him. I used to watch women dealers pay 25 to 50 cents for fine old cut glass, art glass, etc., in the 1960's. They always used to tell me, "If you pay too much for the antiques you are buying, they might not sell you any more later." They will figure, if the antiques are that valuable to a dealer, what are they really worth?

In buying a houseful of antiques, always haul the best ones home with you first on a sweet deal. You can come back for the marginal profit ones the next day. Do not leave one good thing you bought inside the house. Minds are changed in a minute to sell or not to sell, even after you've paid. The judge in these cases rules nine times out of ten for the one who says he sold too cheaply.

When picking auctions to attend, pick those which say "estate sale" on the sale bill. The reason for this is that at other auctions, such as moving sales or any that have the owners' name at the bottom, the best things are held back, and owners are likely to have placed protective bids for other items with the auctioneer that will keep you from getting bargains. But at estate sales, nothing may be held back, and dead persons cannot bid. That is why we all love estate sales.

Another tip, if you intend to go to a flea market, be there the night before it opens when the many-times-novice dealers unpack. A lot of big bargains are bought in this way.

The top advice I can give to the young man or lady who wants to make antique dealing a career is to consider the mail order route. It is the way of the future and avoids packing and unpacking, traveling all over the country to shows, doing bad shows, running the danger of being robbed in strange towns, and many more troublesome things. All you have to do to be a mail-order dealer is place an ad and let it do all the hard work. There is no better way to take an ego trip than to see your name in big block letters over your antique ad. It is this that brought me all the new cars every year, Cap Cod home, and much more. If I had opened up an antique shop, I would never have made it past the first two or three years. I crave antique action when I deal. I want what I buy to sell soon. I don't like to keep anything over a month, and national advertising has done the job for me.

Remember these points:
1. Buy only what you think you can sell.
2. Advertise in your area papers for the antiques you think you know best.
3. Do not give up with your ads. You will sometimes have to run an ad for longer than you care to, but more surely than in Las Vegas when you feed the slot

machine, you will hit the antique jackpot if you are persistent in your advertising. A ton of fine antiques will be kicked out to you. Ads have done this hundreds of times for me. Run ads in as many area and national papers as you can afford to. They will do everything for you I say they will do.

4. Once you buy something, don't run to a local dealer to sell it for 50% of retail. You get a much better price and more quickly nationally than you will staying local, because there is a lot of money out there in the wide open country of Trader-land just waiting to be spent.

Good luck in this fun profession. I will warn you, though, once you get hooked on antiques, you may forget eating and nice clothes. The shabbiest people at sales are often the ones with the best collections.

Antiquing is a little like alchoholism. You become addicted to the lure of finding something new, and you never tire of it.

2

HOW TO BECOME
A SUCCESSFUL
MAIL-ORDER DEALER

So far we have talked mostly about buying. Now we will talk about selling.

Back in 1957 when I first started to advertise my antiques nationally, I was shaking, because although I knew some of my antiques very well, there was a whole gray area where I knew just enough to be dangerous. You must first of all study the antiques you intend to advertise very hard so that you will not be caught sending your customers a mistake, or even worse, a repro. There is nothing that can take the breath out of an aspiring mail-order dealer's lungs any faster than to discover he has mailed a reproduction to a customer.

Years ago I ordered a piece of signed Tiffany that was guaranteed to be as advertised. I couldn't wait until my big bargain would come so I could fall back and chuckle at my luck. The dealer had under-priced the signed Tiffany nine-inch vase at $145 when I knew where I could sell it for $450 with just one phone call. When the box arrived, I opened it hurriedly and saw that the man had mistakenly sent me a nine-inch purple Bohemian swirled glass vase. When I turned it over to see how it was signed and numbered, I saw that a jeweler's tool such as is used to write monograms on gold lockets had been used to forge a Tiffany

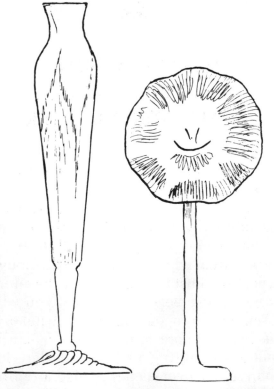

Tiffany vase, 16″, $1,775; jack in the pulpit, 14″, $1,300-$1,400.

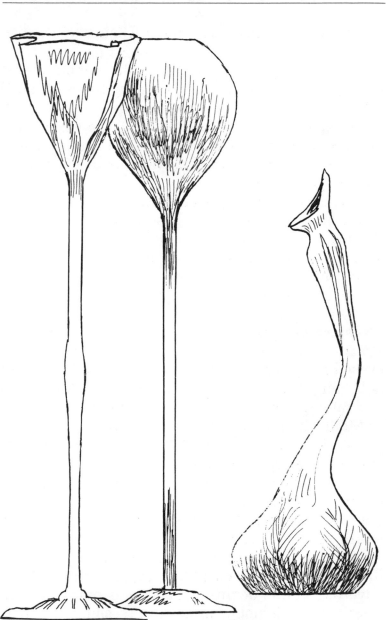

Tiffany vases, flower forms (left and center), 19", $2,000-$2,200; goose neck sprinkler (right), 18", $1,600.

signature, rather than the signature being acid-signed into the base.

I got on the phone and was positive about the indignity, but not too abusive, because I was afraid if I didn't act sweet while being firm in asking for a refund, the dealer might just tell me to go to and stay put. I returned the vase and received the refund, and to this day I have ordered only a smattering of antique art glass by mail.

Be sure you know what is the "real McCoy." If you have the slightest doubt about an item's authenticity, do not attempt to advertise it. Take the questionable piece to a long-established dealer for his opinion. I have found that most reputable dealers feel it quite an honor to be asked if an antique is genuine.

The next thing to do is to pick the correct antique magazine or paper to advertise in. The *Antique Trader* is my best place to sell. I can sell almost everything I advertise there, while an advertiser of dolls might do better in *Hobbies* magazine. I had several years of good luck with *Hobbies* when I was a Mettlach and Royal Doulton specialist. Other possibilities are *Collectors' News, Tri-State Trader* and the magazine, *Antiques*.

I use the scatter-gun approach in the *Trader*. I advertise everything from a wooden zinc-lined bathtub with me sitting in it to a signed Royal Flemish vase worth $2,000 to $3,000.

In writing ads, what has worked for me is to name the fair price I will accept (or pay) for an item. Most advertisers don't do this, but a lot of people won't answer ads that do not name a price. If selling, they may not know what their antiques are worth. If you say you pay $100 for an old quilt or a Shirley Temple doll, they will call you.

To make big money in antiques, you must know how to sell your antique for top bucks. To do this requires a lot of practice. If your antique has a story with it, that story is worth a lot to you.

Since I decided to reveal all my trade secrets in this book and tell it like it is, I will admit that in order to make a prospective buyer come around, most dealers concoct a good story. They employ white lies shamelessly. They will tell you that a pair of signed Tiffany vases came out of the Nelson Rockefeller mansion. (And if they were good enough for billionaire Rockefeller, then you, the buyer, should like them, too.) Or a dining room set came from Pola Negri's estate.

If it is an antique Kentucky rifle, they say it is reputed to have been in the Daniel Boone family. Right away this adds a lot of prestige to the piece, and if it is ever going to be sold, that will do it.

For many years after the Franklin D. Roosevelt stamp auction, his stamps were supposedly being sold by several large eastern stamp companies. They framed a pile of average covers and put his name inside the case. The stamp covers didn't last long, even though it was an outright lie.

The next thing to remember in the mail-order business is to settle all your troubles with your customers yourself. Don't bring the magazine or newspaper staff into the fray except as a last resort. Three X's beside your name in the trouble file of a national magazine, and you'll be out of the antique mail-order business as far as that trade paper is concerned.

This nearly happened in 1962 when I was beginning to emerge into national prominence. I was warned by the editor of a trade magazine that if I couldn't settle my problems alone with my customers, I would lose my advertising privileges. I awoke to the fact that should I lose the papers I advertised in as vehicles to sell my antiques, I would have to start driving spikes on a railroad gang. I chose to straighten up and fly right. From that time 20 years ago, I have had very few problems in the mail-order business that I didn't straighten out quickly.

Once you find the paper or magazine that suits your advertising needs, respect the owner and the staff who work sometimes day and night to see that you get the most for every advertising dollar you spend. It is because your name is in this magazine that people are not afraid to mail you their treasures, and if they are in doubt, they can call the magazine and the staff will vouch for you.

I think mail-order dealing is the only way to go for a young man or woman today, because at any given time with a single ad, you can reach millions of customers. If you set up at a flea market or show, on the other hand, you can display your antiques to only a few hundred people at best. Most of the time, dealers around this area don't sell enough to pay their booth rent at $25.

As you grow in knowledge in the mail-order business, so will your confidence. The more antiques you master, the more of a telephone salesman you will become, and the stronger you will come across.

So, know the antiques you advertise and be able to explain in depth what they are when the phone orders begin to come in. Especially does this hold in the case of dolls. The more you can tell the caller about your sales article, the more he will be inclined to buy it.

3

SHOOTING DOWN HAND-CARVED DUCK DECOYS ALONG THE ILLINOIS RIVER FLYWAY

In 1955 when the decoy-collecting hobby was just getting up a full head of steam, I started advertising to buy old wooden duck decoys. If you weren't a decoy collector at this time, you thought that anybody that bought them had to be a little bit nuts to pay $15 for a nice decoy. I sold a majority of the good ones I scared up to a man from Elgin, Illinois. Bill must have had a lot of experience in buying decoys, because even if I had 300 or 400 primitive-looking hand-carved and hand-painted decoys swimming on my big antique warehouse floor, he would wade through them and buy only six or seven at one time.

They were usually ducks carved by my old friend, Charles Perdew, from Henry, Illinois, and I charged well for them. Charlie used to do the carving while Edna, his wife, did all the beautiful feather painting.

That combination made the Perdew hollow-carved duck decoys worth over $100 even in the late 50's and up through the 60's.

Pintails by Charles Perdew, Henry, Ill., $700-$1,000 each.

The Perdew pintail if in good condition will sell easily today for $1,000 and up if you can find someone who will part with one. The Perdew crow decoy sells for around $600. Old Charlie must have carved a lot of them, because I have bought over a dozen at auctions over the past ten years. Charlie's crow decoys were painted black, and the carved crow feathers were perfection exemplified, his over-all carving making this ugly bird beautiful. The crow decoys had a nail spike on the bottom so they could be stuck on tree branches to attract crows.

Crow shooting was big fun in the fall when I was living on my south Dixon farm. Crows would gather in the three-fourths mile of hedge trees along the Three Mile Branch creek where we had hung 40 or 50 crow decoys. These blackbirds made good pie during the Depression, and believe you me, I have eaten my share of blackbirds baked into a pie. Crows were great destroyers of crops such as corn, and also carried animal diseases on their feet as they lit in barnyards.

Charles Perdew also carved wooden duck calls. They were carefully carved and then equally beautifully painted by Edna. I used to see them for sale in the Henry stores in the 30's for only a few dollars. Recently I heard that a Henry man witnessed a collector pull out six $100 bills for a Perdew duck call, but the would-be seller turned the out-of-town buyer down.

During the past ten years Charlie's son has also been carving decoys with workmanship that makes him a close rival to his father. He signs his name on a metal tag so his work will not be confused with his father's.

At the recent five-day Princeton auction I attended, Charlie's decoys would have brought a record price if there had been any there. The premier grade Detroit hand-carved decoys sold there easily for $1,000 each. Ordinary Illinois Flyway duck decoys hovered around the $500 and $600 mark all through the bidding on 50 or 60 decoys. To the 400 people seated there, the decoy buyers must have seemed nuts, especially when they would buy a premier Detroit decoy for $1,000 and hug it to their stomachs and smile ear-to-ear while holding their bid number in the air all the while they were bidding to show they meant business and were going to buy more at that price. The old-time decoy collectors just stood back and watched in disbelief.

When I saw those prices, I knew I should have kept all the thousands of decoys that in the late 50's and 60's I sold either to local buyers or through my national ads.

In 1964 I went to visit the great Peru, Illinois,

decoy carver and painter, Fred Destri, because I had heard through the decoy grapevine that he had a pair of Charles Walker duck decoys to sell. Walker, the king of all Illinois carvers, had lived in Princeton 1876-1954. He was to me the greatest of all the 100 or more Illinois Flyway carvers that are scattered from LaSalle-Peru past Bureau and Princeton, then sprinkled past Henry to the Mississippi River. While Charles Perdew carved 20,000 decoys in his lifetime from 1900 to 1962, Charles Walker carved just 75 dozen. Walker's feather painting on his 75 dozen equals a DaVinci oil painting in my book. The duck decoy collector today lives for the chance that someday, somewhere, he will be able to buy a decoy carved by Charles Walker. I can always say I had my chance and missed it.

Destri first showed me the beautiful decoys he was carving and painting, which he would sell for $75 each. The Destri trademark was the completely turned head with the bill nestling on the back feathers.

I was then invited to his basement, and there sitting alone on some shelves was the greatest pair of decoys I had ever seen. They were the broad-billed Charles Walkers that I had heard were on sale at Destri's. I quickly asked how much they were. Destri answered coolly, "$2,500 for the pair." I would have bought them, except the mallard was worth only half as much as a Walker pintail at that time, so I thanked Destri and drove back home, wondering even then if I had made a big mistake. I found out soon enough I should have bought them, because just a year or two later the same pair of decoys sold for $3,000.

The way I would buy duck decoys along the Illinois River Flyway in those early years was to place innocuous-sounding ads in the papers of all the Illinois river towns all the way to the Mississippi, and at times north to Dubuque, Iowa. I often hit the duck decoy "mother lode" where I could buy right and sell right.

One memorable time I was called to the small Mississippi River town of Albany by a letter. The 1967 letter said, in response to my ad, "I am retired and have some duck decoys for sale." The letter was signed with a telephone number.

I am not an experienced advertiser for nothing. I knew as soon as I read this short letter with the shaky handwriting that I would buy some great duck decoys there. I called for directions, and as darkness came on, I arrived at a modest little home along the Mississippi River. My heart was now starting to pound as I got out of my car and walked swiftly to the small barn in the back where I had been told to go. I knocked on the barn door, and a squatty old man who was wearing a river boat captain's hat admitted me to his decoy room.

I couldn't believe what I saw. This man wasn't carving wooden duck decoys as I assumed he was from our phone conversation. He was making duck decoys and yard ornaments, out of all things, plastic. I asked him quite angrily why he didn't say he had plastic ducks to sell and not wooden ones like I had asked for in my ad.

Then came the biggest thrill and shock of my entire 50-year advertising career. The old man said he was a retired Mississippi River boat captain, and in the winters back in the 30's he had carved around 200 or 300 wooden duck decoys that he couldn't sell because they were over-sized. Living on the rough Mississippi, he had made his decoys one and a half times bigger than normal so that they would not move back and forth in the rough river water. This made them almost impossible to sell, he found, so he stopped carving them. He mentioned around 15 or 20 carvers whom he said were much better carvers than himself and whose decoys were better adapted to the more tranquil waters of the Illinois River.

I asked him if he had any of the over-sized decoys left. A man is entitled to one great thrill in his life and I got it. The wizened old captain motioned to a ladder halfway back in his barn, and without even looking in that direction, pointed his gnarled finger and said, "They're up there."

I nearly fell off the ladder climbing the eight or nine rungs to the loft, but it would have been worth it if I had only had one look and then fallen and broken my neck. There, faintly, I could see row on row of some of the greatest hand-carved and hand-painted mallard and pintail decoys that God could ever give a nutty decoy dealer the right to see. I brought one down with me, and I could savor just buying that one, let alone the whole barn loft full.

I had said in my ad, as I always used to say when advertising for decoys, that I wanted to buy a few duck decoys to go hunting with in the fall. I never once intimated I was dealing in them. If I had done this, not one man or woman would have sold me their duck decoys, because there was a lot of sentiment involved with decoys--all the good old days spent duck hunting, etc. Decoy owners would much rather sell them to a fellow duck hunter who could use them, than to sell even a splinter to a "scalper" or antique dealer who might make money on them.

I thought as I came down the ladder with one of the best pintail duck decoys in my hand, "how am I

Oversize mallard decoys by an unknown Albany, Ill., carver, circa 1930's, $500 a pair.

going to buy what I saw in that loft? There must be hundreds of them sitting up there covered with a layer of dust from being there 35 years."

I asked the captain, who was busy finishing up a plastic shore duck silhouette, if he would sell me some of his old over-sized decoys. This is when I got the second biggest shock of my career. He said, "I'll sell them all for $5 each, but that means you're going to have to buy them all. I don't know how you intend to use them. They're too darn big."

I calmly agreed to his $5-take-all terms, and backed my van up to the barn door. I worked as fast as possible to get the around-200 mint decoys loaded, and went up and down that ladder that night faster than I ever thought I could. All this time the river boat captain kept right on working on his plastic decoys. For every one of the great hand-carved decoys I was loading, he would have to make a barrel of plastic ones to equal the price I figured each of the beautiful decoys would bring.

After almost an hour of bringing down decoys and marking each on a piece of paper the captain had put up, the total duck decoy bag that night came to 187. I paid the $5 each and left town.

The thing I always remember is how the captain kept down-grading the work he had done years before. This is always a big pry in buying something, if the item is not wanted. You can almost steal a signed Tiffany lamp if the owner hates it.

When I started in selling the captain's decoys, they sold like hotcakes for $200 a pair to everybody I knew that collected decoys.

The entire length of the big Illinois River Flyway was loaded with prolific decoy carvers during the Depression. The Flyway is where the ducks migrating south in the Fall stop to eat corn out of the fields along the river and rest for the next lap of the journey.

Never again will we see such an abundance of art work concentrated in so small an area. Every town along the Illinois River teemed with these great artists in wood and paint.

Peru, Illinois, carvers included Henry Gross, August Esmond, Samuel Hocking, Sr., Samuel Hocking, Jr., Leopold Koehler, George Koehler, Chris

Powers, Hermon Reitgrof, Fred Weber, and Charles Gisler. Peru is a great town even today in which to place a wanted-to-buy decoy ad.

For my bucks, Hector Whittington, from Oglesby, Illinois, carved some of the best decoys. Robert Bradbeer, Thomas Chiado, Oscar Peterson, Mono Pilotti, and Michael Vallero are all Spring Valley carvers. A few miles down river was Robert Elliston, Bureau, Illinois. Elliston's decoys are selling 'way up there in the hundreds, and there is no stopping them from breaking the $1,000 barrier in the future.

I bought and sold almost every one of the decoys I am naming at one time or another when I was known as "Quack-Quack" Shiaras by all my dealer friends. If they laughed, it wouldn't have been for long if they knew how much one trip to Albany cleared for me.

When buying decoys, buy only the carved out, hollow ones. You can tell if they are hollow by looking for a seam along the sides where the carver glued the top half onto the hollowed-out bottom half. They are much lighter than the solid-wood decoys. Another thing to look for is whether the decoy has its original, fine paint. If you are suspicious of the decoy being a repaint, stay away; unless, of course, the decoy is a Charles Perdew or a Charles Walker. Then buy it.

The feather painting is of the utmost importance to me. In buying decoys I have used the buying approach that I have used successfully in other lines. If the decoy doesn't speak to me, then I forget it. It has to have this much and more to the party who might purchase it from you. Besides, it is easier to sell something you like than something you don't like.

Happy decoy hunting. It could make you rich overnight.

Top left, 17" Steiner, $3,000-$3,500; right, 27" Bru Jne R 12, $10,000-$12,000; bottom, 26" Jumeau, $5,500-$6,500.

4

MY FRENCH DOLL CONNECTION

In the mid-60's before the antique doll craze, Fran and I had a nice sideline going buying French dolls from the Madame Maraud Doll Studios in Paris, then selling them around the country through national ads. We would write Madame Maraud that we wanted to buy about 100 dolls and, in return, would receive several large glossy pictures, each showing about 20 numbered Steiner and Jumeau dolls. On an accompanying piece of green tissue paper were descriptions.

The dolls were priced from $125 to $175 each. Fran would do the choosing because she was going to sell many of them privately as well as through our ads. If she liked a doll in a photo, she could always do a good job of selling it.

The doll descriptions read something like this:

Steiner 26", blue paperweight eyes, LaParisienne leather body, pierced ears, natural hair blond wig, bisque head with bisque swivel shoulder plate body, bisque hands, and closed mouth, $165.

Jumeau 21″, brown natural hair, brown paper-weight eyes, closed mouth, pierced ears, creamy complexion, bisque socket head with bisque swivel plate body, $185.

From the hundreds of dolls in Madame Maraud's photos, we would usually order 75 or 80, trying to keep our order down to $10,000, which was a big amount of money to spend on dolls in those days. About a month after we had sent our order, a letter would advise us that our doll order was ready to be shipped via surface freight to Chicago's Navy Pier as soon as she received the money. Madame Maraud did not trust airplanes with her valuable dolls.

We would receive notification as soon as our containers arrived and we would drive to Navy Pier to start hunting for them among the hundreds of boxes there. Sometimes this search would take the whole day; but in the end we would locate the boxes and take the beautiful French dolls back to Dixon for national advertisement and (hopefully) profitable sale.

By 1966 the doll business ended for us because of prices that tripled and quadrupled in only a few years. The demand simply surpassed the supply of fine French dolls in this country, and when this happens in anything, prices go sky-high overnight.

Prices today at doll sales may run as high as $31,000 for the 16″ French Bru, which brought that at a Sotheby auction in 1982. French Brus commonly sell now for $8,000 and $12,000, while Jumeaus and Steiners run a close second. Usually they will sell quickly for $5,000 to $8,000 to both men and women bidders who are socking them away as good investments.

At the turn of the century, these dolls were sold

by New York city's big department stores. No sooner would newspaper ads announce that two or three thousand French dolls had arrived for sale at $2.50 each, when a mad rush of buyers would descend on the store and buy the dolls in only a few hours. The French Steiner, Jumeau, and Bru dolls were much in demand, and today, almost a hundred years later, there is an even stronger demand. I personally think this demand will always be present. Many men as well as women derive a great deal of satisfaction from gazing at the timeless, beautiful expressions on the dolls' faces put there by the doll makers of long ago.

I used to love to go into dusty, creepy attics in the 60's to see if a really good doll might be lying in the dust instead of just an average one such as I used to buy for next to nothing. I bought them not only complete, but, if I could get them, a bushel full of heads, bodies, and loose eyes in all sizes for only a few bucks. Then I would sell them through picture ads reading "Dolls by the bushel--$150," and make good money.

One day I got a call from twin sisters--Lola and Lila--saying they had some dolls and some antiques for sale. When I got to their home I was escorted up into their attic, which was so full of treasures that I had to walk around sideways.

When I asked where the dolls were, the sisters motioned with gnarled fingers loaded with diamonds and opals to a four-drawer oak chest. I had to part a few streamers of cobwebs to get to it. As I pulled the top drawer open, I had a seizure of shortness of breath to see three pair of French closed-mouth bisque dolls lying asleep next to each other, dressed in all the finery that money could buy little girls. They were 18 to 20" dolls worth several hundred dollars apiece.

I guessed then that all the dolls I would be shown, would be twins. The two girls were daughters of a rich judge who had lavished the best on them, going to Marshall Field's in Chicago at Christmas each year, bringing back the finest in French dolls. The girls had never married, and so had no children to wear out their dolls. Now they were selling everything so they would know where their family treasures had gone.

The other three drawers of the chest contained several more pair of rare French dolls. I ended up buying them all at my price. I also bought all the sisters' art glass, oriental rugs, and beautiful walnut, marble-topped furniture. But where the fun really was, was in that dust-filled attic. I found more fine old dolls and mint toys there than I was able to find during the next 20 years.

When I got the dolls home, I kept them for almost a year. As much as I like live dolls, these took precedence. I look at them as works of art. Each German or French doll company had its own idea of how to make dolls, and the dolls made by each had their own expression. Today, this expression can extract money right out of old gray-haired ladies' pockets.

As a lover of old dolls, I didn't want to sell these; but one day I needed some money. I called a doll-collecting couple in Sterling to come and see them. The couple said they didn't have any money, but they found the money when they saw the dolls.

This doll and antique bonanza was the result of a local newspaper ad which I placed. I didn't run into it by going to garage sales. It is in the attics of your own hometown that French and German dolls may be lying, waiting for you to open a door and find them there.

5

THE MAN WHO MISTOOK
A RARE DRY SINK
FOR A CALF BUNK

A dry sink, as everyone knows by now, is not a sink that's out of water, but a wooden sink which Great-grandmother did her dishes in. It was usually made of pine and had a well to hold the dishes. Commonly it had two doors below and a single shelf above.

The rarest dry sink is the high-backed kind that has around a two and one-half foot back, with two or three drawers across the top. This sink brings $750 to $800, while the low-backed kind sells for $300 to $400. In 1974 my student partner found and bought seven high-backed dry sinks, all within six weeks, and neither of us has seen one for sale since.

Not too long before this happened, I had agreed to teach what I knew about antiques to a young salesman, Nate Ross. Nate wasn't what you would call a green-horn. He had a few fine old primitive chests and cupboards in his home. I had instructed him in what to look for in primitives, as well as in furniture like Chippendale, Hepplewhite, and Queen Anne, in case a city piece should turn up. I warned him to be careful in dealing for dry sinks, as the carpenters of Wisconsin are busy all winter when they can't work outdoors making "old-appearing early American" pine furniture out of old barn lumber, complete with square nails. If you are even semi-green, you can really get burned to the tune of $700 and up.

I told Nate to be on the look-out for a great old dry sink with high back that was rumored to be in the Polo area 10 miles to the north of us. It was supposed to have drawers with white porcelain pulls all across the top.

Not long after this conversation, Nate heard a couple of dealers mention that an old farmer near Polo had an old high cupboard in his barn that they would like to buy, but he wouldn't sell it. Nate caught just the name "Alex." He took off for Polo at the first opportunity. Since Polo is a small town, he soon ran into someone who knew an Alex and directed him down the road a few miles.

When Nate drove into Alex Ruff's farmyard in his old maroon pick-up truck he felt his heart pounding in wild anticipation of making a great score in this farmer's barn, but outwardly he acted calm and nonchalant. He found Alex outside at his hog feeder working the feed down. Alex came over and asked Nate what he could do for him, and Nate asked him if he happened to have any old furniture he wanted to sell, explaining that he and his bride were just setting up housekeeping and would like to do it with old furniture that they could refinish themselves.

Alex said he didn't have any old furniture. But since he and his wife were long-time lamp collectors-- in fact they had often bought lamps from me--he and Nate got started talking shop. After about two hours of it, Nate had toured all the out-buildings except one.

Finally Nate asked Alex if he had anything in the barn.

"Go ahead and look," said Alex, "but there ain't nothin' in there you'd want."

The first thing Nate saw when he walked in the barn were two white knobs sticking out of a big pile of loose hay. He asked Alex what kind of an object that was with the white knobs. Alex took a pitchfork and lifted off the hay to reveal what Nate thought was the most beautiful dry sink he had ever seen.

"What is that piece of furniture used for?" Nate asked.

Alex said something then that was unbelieveable. He said, "This is a calf feeder trough that my grand-dad brought from Pennsylvania. You just dump a bucket or two of corn and oats in the trough there, and the calves eat it. It's just the right height for a feed bunk, too," Alex added as he pointed his finger at the dry sink's well.

"That might fit good in my kitchen," Nate said. "How much do you want for it?"

"Well, a few years ago, an antique dealer from Mt. Morris offered me $30 for it, but I didn't take it."

Just then Alex took hold of what turned out to be another dry sink hidden in the hay, and dragged it in-to the open beside the big Pennsylvania beauty, and that is when dry-sink-buying history was made.

Nate offered Alex triple what the other dealer had, $90 for the high-backed sink and $45 for the smaller

Rare painted Pennsylvania dry sink with finger and sponge graining, circa 1820, $2,000. An unusual feature is the down-turned horseshoes, bad luck according to Pennsylvania Dutch tradition.

one. Nate almost passed out when his offer was accepted. He hurried to load the sinks in his truck with Alex's help, fearful that at any moment, Mrs. Ruff, who had gone to town, might come back and queer the deal.

A little later, when Nate drove into my farmyard honking his horn, with the high sink standing up in the back of his truck, I could hardly believe my eyes. It was the most beautiful dry sink I had ever seen and was everything I had heard. There on its four top drawers were the four white porcelain knobs I had told Nate to look for. Each knob was surrounded by a small carved wooden horseshoe. The splashboard of the sink, below the high drawers, was painted dark blue, as was the inside of the well. The drawers were sponge-grained with brown paint, while the rest of the wood was finger-grained. A carved wooden horseshoe decorated each of the lower doors, and the whole bottom of the piece was scalloped.

When I got over the shock of seeing this important Pennsylvania dry sink, I took a look at the other one. It was the low pine kind, but still very beautiful and valuable.

I had asked Nate if I could have first chance to buy the only piece of primitive pine furniture that I had ever felt I had to have. I preferred the pre-1800 city furniture with its graceful proportions and slender, inlaid legs.

"You didn't think I was going to leave here with it, did you?" Nate asked. With that we gently unloaded the rare sink. The next problem was where to put it, as our house was packed so full of furniture, glass, and lamps that we could not have forced in another piece. My wife, Fran, and I decided to leave the Ruff's dry sink out on our porch on a temporary basis.

There it stood for around two months before I found some good lamps to sell the Ruffs. I called them, telling them what I had bought, and asked them to drive down after chores and see them. They said it would be nearly dark before they could make it. I told Fran to put a cover over the dry sink so they would not see it, since Nate had told them he was going to put it in his house.

Fran covered the sink to please me, but privately she had made other plans.

I learned later that Fran still had in mind how the Ruffs had come to our house on several occasions to buy lamps, and had repeatedly tried to buy a pull-down lamp with pink mother-of-pearl shade and rows of prisms that we had hanging in our living room and that she was especially fond of. They finally talked me out of it for $575, much against Fran's will. Later, when they visited us again, they boasted, "We did good on that lamp. We sold it for $1,400."

So as the Ruffs drove up, Fran, unbeknown to me, took the cover off the sink and turned on the porch light to show it off better.

I walked out to greet my good friends and best lamp buyers, when, as Mrs. Ruff stepped on the porch, she turned to Alex and said, "Why, Alex, isn't that your grandfather's dry sink?"

When Alex admitted that it was, I jumped in the conversation quickly and told them a guy named Nate Ross had traded it to me for some oriental rugs.

Alex, who was a quiet man with a trusting nature, having lived close to the soil all his life, was even quieter than usual that night. Everything was as if we were at a friend's wake. Only this time it was the loss of the big four-drawer, high-backed, blue interior deep well, finger-grain-painted Pennsylvania dry sink that was the cause for deep sadness.

That night the Ruffs stayed only a short time, and it was the last time I was to see them as customers. Maybe a brief hello at sales, but no longer were we friends.

Nate and I went on to buy five or more high-backed dry sinks in less than six weeks, which is a record for those days. They sold for an average of $500 each. We will always remember the big one that pales all others, bought for $90 and worth $2,500 to $3,000 then in 1973.

The one thing we could never figure out even after hashing and rehashing this story, was how a man like Alex, who had been buying and selling antique lamps for a long time, could call the greatest piece of Pennsylvania Dutch primitive furniture ever to surface in the Midwest a feed bunk. I always was meaning to ask him about this, but thought better of it.

Monmouth Pottery Sleepy Eye stein in blue and gray, $450; brown and tan, $1,000; 1 qt. pitcher in blue and white, $125-$135. Both circa 1900-1920.

6

AROUND THE STATES
IN FIVE DAYS
WITH AN AD

If you want to be a mail-order dealer, the Number 1 thing is to know what you are advertising backwards and forwards. When responses to your ads start coming in, the callers will want to know all about the antiques you have advertised in the trade magazines. I studied antiques at least ten years before I got nerve enough to run an ad, and then it was a small one!

Having a national outlet through ads is a big advantage. In some instances I can pay 50% over what other dealers would pay for articles, since I can sell to the nation. They must sell to a limited number of local collectors and dealers.

After I have spent two or three weeks getting good antiques bought at right prices, I make a list of them, with the ones I want to photograph, probably 15, at the top of my list. Then I go around the house and photograph them with my Polaroid camera. I give each photo a number. Then I type up an ad listing about 80 items, with the 15 pictures and the rest only numbered and described. The ad is apt to take a full page and cost about $550.

Everything in my ad is priced. I don't like a bit those blind-price ads about which you are forced to call long distance at great expense, only to find that an antique you can normally buy for $100 is priced at $200.

I try to start my ad with something funny that has happened to me. I may also interject some humor in the middle to keep the reader reading. At the end I often put in a corny question and answer exchange.

In about ten days after I mail or call in my ad, I begin to get calls from all parts of the nation. Fairbanks, Alaska, wants to buy some old cast iron pots and pans that I periodically advertise for dealers there, who tell me they are still commonly used to cook with on cast iron stoves. The California dealers call for $250-to-$300 quilts or marble turtle-top tables. With California a late-settled state, dealers there buy a lot of good and very bad antiques at ridiculously high prices.

My callers seldom hang up before a half-hour is up. The Californians tell me the market is slow for average antiques, but good for fine ones. They introduce me to new money-making items, like old hand-made rag rugs. Out there they sell for $15 to $25, while here they go begging at most sales.

I then get a call from outside the New Orleans harbor, as a barge captain orders a hundred different tobacco plug tags while piloting his barge out into the Gulf of Mexico.

My next caller is from New Jersey. I cause him to nearly drop over when I guess his state after I hear him speak a word or two. Next is a Brooklyn caller, whose Brooklynese it takes a special language course to understand.

In my business, I felt a loss of revenue about one and a half years ago from states east of the Mississippi, due to high interest rates that put the economy on a down-trend. My ads containing around 100 antiques items used to sell out 75%, which is darned good considering my customers are buying an antique without seeing it. Then my business fell to 50% of normal, with 95% of the buyers now being from west of the Mississippi.

What a rat race it is when each part of the country starts to phone me about a really low-priced antique I have for sale! If you want to hear the phone ring day and night, just price a rare tobacco tin or fine old quilt (which you have pictured) too low. You are completely free of phone troubles if it is too high.

From the "Catbird Seat" in Grand Detour, I am able to monitor exactly what is going on in the antique world by the response to my national ads. Unfortunately, trade papers cannot hit every part of the country on the same day. Editors will never know the static I take from people who have just received their papers and call up to buy a coveted antique, only to find someone in another area who got his paper the day before has beaten them to it.

Now my phones are beginning to stop ringing, so I know it has to be Friday, and my big ad which came out on Monday has run its course. There won't be any more phones ringing day and night in my house until my next ad comes out.

Some "sleepers" that can make you money: doorstop, $75; Christmas tree ornaments, $20; Case knife, $100-$2,500; corkscrew, $75; 5-hook lure, $20.00.

7

SLEEPING UNDER THE DOUBLE EAGLE, KING OF ORIENTAL RUGS

In the spring of 1975, I drove to an antique sale in Freeport, Illinois, a town of around 28,000 people whose red brick Civil War-era homes along Stephenson Street were known to be loaded up to their attics with fine antiques and oriental rugs. The sale on that Saturday turned out to be on a short side street running off from Stephenson Street, and at as poor a looking house for Freeport's better section as I have ever seen.

Another minus that day was the fact that the auctioneer, Wally Worthen, worked closely with dealer Fred Knight. Knight, from nearby Milledgeville, is considered by many to be the greatest antique dealer alive today. He has been working at the trade with his mother ever since just a baby, and has kept right on going.

But Knight and I each had our own greatness that

day when I was to make oriental rug history and out-
wit the Worthen-Knight combination.

We got there late with everything sold but two
rugs, one four by six feet, and the other five and one-
half by eight and one-half. I almost fell over when I
saw that the smaller one, lying on the grass, was a double eagle Kazak that I knew had to be good from study-
ing the pictures every month in the magazine **Antiques**. Advertisers don't place even a small rug ad in
this magazine without its costing $300 to $400.

I pointed the rug out to my wife, and told her, "It's
a double eagle Kazak that I just have to have. How do
I go about buying it with Fred Knight already in on
it, or both him and Worthen, who knows?"

I was afraid that if I ever tried to second-guess
Fred in person, or when he had left a secret bid with
no ceiling, I'd be wasting my time.

The rarest rug was pointed to, then, as it lay on
the grass. The bidding got started at a fast pace, with
my taking it up to just under $400, when I dropped
out. Worthen would not be impressed enough by this
price, I figured, to call Fred afterward and tell him
the rug had to be a good piece because I was there
and bid it up to $700 or $800. I knew the rug would
be mine, anyway, before the night was over.

I was good on oriental rugs at that time, but by
no means an expert. I just fooled around with orientals as a sideline, because they were no longer cheap,
as in the late 1950's and all through the 60's, when
I could buy a great, room-size oriental carpet worth
$6,000 for $2,000, or a commoner $800 Sarouk carpet
for $50.

I threw a few hard bids at the other, large burnt-
orange-on-rusty-red rug, and then let it go.

Since I was not absolutely sure who had bought the great early 1800's northwest-Persia double eagle Kazak and the burnt orange rug, I slipped a $20 bill to a helper of Worthen's to tell me who the tough opposition was that day. I said to him, "Fred Knight was the bidder of the rugs today, wasn't he, Clint?"

With $20 in his hand, Clint said, "Yes. Fred was here yesterday and left a bid of $675 on the smaller one and $700 on the bigger rug."

This is what $20 can buy you in Freeport. It can and did buy me $6,000 worth of rugs for a few old pieces of pine furniture.

I got home and made a call to my antique student, Nate Ross, who was also a picker or supplier for Fred Knight of dry sinks and all the rest in primitive furniture that Fred could refinish and retail out of his shop. I told Nate what had happened in Freeport, that the rarest Persian rug I had ever seen had been at the sale, and I had let Fred Knight's "buy" bidder get it with a proxy bid of $450. This rug could be sold for at least $4,000 to a customer of mine who collected the type of weave found in it. I explained to Nate it was circa 1800 Persian rug weaving at its best. The other rug was an old Caucasian, too, and also mint. "If I had only known what Knight's bid was," I told Nate, "I could possibly have taken the rugs home right away by outbidding him." But Knight was known not to stop bidding for things he wanted.

"Call Fred and tell him this story," I said to Nate. "Tell him you got to the sale just as they had finished selling the two rugs, which you had wanted to buy, and that you learned they had been sold to him. Tell Fred you know how much he bought them for, and

The 4′ x 6′ Double Eagle Kazak, $5,500-$6,500.

you will double his money in dry sinks or in a cupboard or two.

"Don't wait for Fred to drive up to Freeport to pay
and pick up the rare double eagle," I said, "or it will
be curtains. He will never get it once he takes it back
to Milledgeville. He will call up one of his oriental rug
expert friends in Chicago, and when they tell him it
is one of the rarest oriental rugs in all the country, he
will price it accordingly."

Nate did as I told him, and the trade was struck
with Knight at 5:30 p.m. that Saturday. Nate took off
for Freeport at high speed to retrieve the rugs that we
hoped would make us a serious profit before the night
was over. In the meantime, I called my Persian rug
buyers in Chicago.

By 8:30 p.m. Nate had reached home with the
rugs, and called me.

"Are you sure," Nate asked, "that you know what
you're doing? The bigger one has a hole in it. I traded
Fred a lot of good furniture for those rugs."

"Stay cool and hang in there, Nate," I told him.
"I'll be right over for a look. Our rug buyers from
Chicago will be there soon. When they heard I had
an eagle Kazak and one more rug to sell, they said
they'd drive straight over to your house."

While Nate and I stood around nervously waiting
for our buyers, I related to Nate how I met them at
a party the year before, and they had asked me to keep
an eye open for early Caucasian oriental rugs, very
primitive-looking and circa 1840. While we paced nervously back and forth trying to figure out what price
to ask, I picked up the eagle Kazak and went over to
the big davenport and lay down, covering myself with
the most valuable rug, as far as I know, ever to have

been sold to anyone in the Midwest up to that day (and probably up to now, seven years later). I covered myself with it, and for a short time I snoozed under the warmth of the double eagle.

Shortly a knock came at the door, and Nate invited the rug buyers, a man and his wife, to come in. They both liked the rugs. Nate, sitting in the next room while the dealing when on, heard me ask $4,000 for the two together. When the couple said they'd buy them, Nate had to stifle, first a gasp, and then laughter of happiness.

The current value of a fine Kazak double eagle rug is now $5,000 to $6,000. To think I sold one for $3,000 five years ago!

When the Chicago couple had paid me for the rugs, I asked them what the larger rug with the hole was. They told me that rug was also an early 19th Century Kazak! They said such rugs often have the old burnt orange coloring and soft reds seen in that rug. I knew then I had just made a monumental boo-boo. The larger rug, as big a Kazak as it was, and with all its geometric design done in early weaving, was worth as much as the rare double eagle. Nate and I had just kissed $3,000 good-bye.

I heard through a rug dealer on Chicago's Michigan Avenue that the next day our Kazak rug buyers had been in his shop trying to sell our two Kazaks for $8,000. They probably sold them for close to that down the street at the biggest and oldest rug shop in Chicago.

8

GRANDMA'S GAY NINETIES
QUILT -- THE 1980's
BEST INVESTMENT

Although I do not have the ability to work with my hands, I love beautiful hand-made objects such as oriental rugs, Indian rugs, Indian baskets, fine Persian tapestries, and most of all, quilts. About 1955 I decided I would deal in some of these articles.

The large supply of quilts that I found, then, at almost all estate sales, and their comparatively cheap price in comparison to other antiques, made the hobby of collecting and showing quilts a lot of fun. When I started, there was no competition to speak of. By 1961-62 I already had over 300 never-used applique and Civil War-era show quilts in my rapidly growing collection that was the talk of antique shows in my area.

At that time I was buying rare quilts for under $25. Once at Lena, Illiois, near Freeport, I found 51 never-

used antique quilts, all at one auction. I had driven
to the sale spurred on by an ad in the Freeport paper.
After travelling back roads, I finally located it at a big
imperious-looking, ante-bellum home hid in a grove
of trees. When I drove up, there was already a large
crowd of sales-goers ahead of me who were, as always
at the hundreds of sales I have attended, one-tenth
buyers and the rest gawkers who monopolize the front
row.

The first thing I saw when I walked into the yard
was a lot of marble-topped walnut furniture that many
times in those days went for a few dollars. I watched
at this sale as a tall, walnut Lincoln-sized bed and an
equally beautiful matching marble-topped dresser with
a high marble splashboard commode could not even
raise a starting bid. I will never forget what happened next. The auctioneer announced then that he would
sell the three-piece set for three times the highest bid.
A bid of only $1 was made, and after begging for more
and not getting it, the auctioneer sold the set for $3.

In those days, old furniture of that period was just
that. Collectors didn't want it in their homes at that
time in our antique collecting history.

But what I had driven 60 miles to buy were the
few old quilts listed on the sale bill. I knew the auctioneer was apt to represent things wrong in his sales
ads, so "a few" might mean two or 100.

Since the quilts were not in sight yet, I asked if
I could see them prior to their being put outside. I hate
to inspect antiques of any kind when competitors are
looking. It is likely to tip them off that I want
something that up until then, they are only mildly interested in, and this could turn them into a hive full
of bidding hornets. When at a sale, look but do not

touch and give away your hand, is my rule.

I was escorted into the house and shown two large wooden boxes in the front room. When I pried the first one open, I fell back in amazement, because I had a glimpse of as gorgeous an early quilt as any I had by then in my 300-quilt, show-quality collection. As I went quickly through both boxes, I counted 51 fine, circa 1890 handmade quilts, with most still showing the quilter's pencil marks.

All of the quilts were then hung outside on a long clothesline. As the sale was about to get started, a friend of mine heard one of my lady competitors say, referring to me, "Why couldn't he have gotten killed on the way up here?"' This is how fierce the competition for good quilts had gotten by that time.

I didn't stick around for the quilt auction. I left my foster son to bid for me. I told Ed, who was only 16 at the time, how far to go on all 51 quilts.

"Go ahead to your other sale, Dad, and make some good buys," Ed said.

I circled back to Freeport and bought several good things to list in my weekly ad. When I drove back to the Lena sale, there sat Ed looking very downhearted and dejected, as if he had not bought even one quilt. When I asked how things had gone, he stood up and smiled.

"Sure, Dad, I bought them all," he said. "I paid $10 or $20 more for the best ones, and I didn't let Rose (my competitor) get even one."

We loaded up the quilts that I had paid a then-record price for of $50 average. I knew that with these high prices, the end had come for the big Midwest quilt give-away. From the day of this early 1960's quilt auction until now, fine hand-made quilts and rugs

One of a pair of Eagle quilts, circa 1875. Eagles face in different directions. Value for the pair, $2,750-$3,000.

have increased 100-fold in value.

In 1970 my quilt collection had gone over the 1,000 mark, with an investment of under $25,000. These $1,000 quilts were all mint with top workmanship. In the 60's I used to show but not sell 200 or more quilts at our annual antique show, hanging them from wall to wall at the show's entrance. Older women used to gather in knots around the different quilts to talk about them and explain to one another how each was made.

I got tired of my quilt hobby in 1973, and sold out just before quilts took their big price jump to where today it is not uncommon for me to pay $150 for a good quilt and $750 up for a patriotic flag quilt or scenic.

The highest priced quilt I have ever bid on was sold last year, 1982, at an auction next to my home in Grand Detour. I bid $750 on a fine World War I patriotic quilt and was outbid by a local man.

My quilt collection was sold through my national ad in 1974, to a large quilt dealer in the East. She said she believed the collection was the very best in the country at that time.

To have good re-sale value, a quilt must be pre-1940. In buying, check the material to be sure it is not post-1940's wash-and-wear. Wash-and-wear material used to piece a quilt is as a red flag to a bull where pros are concerned. Early fabrics give a bedroom the quaint, early look the true purist collector demands. Such a mint quilt is currently bringing at the large national quilt shows $600 low and $3,500 high. At an auction recently in Sotheby Parke Bernet's New York galleries, a group of early Amish quilts sold in the range of $8,000 to $11,000 each.

When you are looking for a quilt to buy, check to be

certain that it is hand-made and not machine-made. A machine-made quilt may be very beautiful, but since comparatively few work hours have gone into its making, it isn't even worth $10 to the pro who buys and sells quilts for a living.

Next, check to see that there aren't any spots, stains, or tears on the quilt. Spots are sure death to its value if you wish to sell it.

As already mentioned, be sure the quilt is not made of wash-and-wear material. If it is, then it is no more than 40 years old and not an antique. 1940-era quilts will never go any higher, whereas the 1930 and earlier quilts are going up every day, in contrast to the downward trend of some other collectibles.

One more thing to watch for, stay away from a single-bed quilt unless it is one of a pair. A pair of single-bed antique quilts is a very good investment any time.

Lastly, and a very important thing to watch for, is the manner in which the quilter did her stitching. The fancier the scrolls, fans, swirls, and other devices used in the quilting, the more valuable the quilt. The stitches themselves should be small and close together.

It took the women of the early 1900's on an average of three or four months to complete a quilt. You can see why they are still a good investment at $250 to $300 each.

9

MADAME X'S
TIFFANY
WISTERIA

When I walk up to an auction, other dealers in many instances become terrified and go back home. This may sound like braggadocio, but it is the truth, and a long time ago I, too, felt the very same fear as I faced the better-known dealers of the 50's. They could chew you up and spit you out when there was something good at stake.

Dealers are not exactly a friendly fraternity. All the antique dealers I know are very jealous of one another. Most can't sleep after losing an antique to another buyer.

Of course we have our "pickers," whom we cooperate with. Grace Bennett appeared to be just another elderly housewife as we began to talk at a Freeport, Illinois, sale a few years ago. After we had visited awhile, she asked me if I would like her to keep me informed about antique sales in her area and people who had antiques for sale. I told her I would pay her a 10% finder's fee for this. It was Grace who would lead me on the great Freeport L. C. Tiffany Wisteria Lamp Chase.

Grace got me on the phone collect only a few days after our first meeting, and told me that she knew a lady with a set of Haviland for sale. The date was set to look at it, and after I had driven up and paid $600 for the Haviland, I met Grace and peeled off her $60 finder's fee.

Around a month passed, during which time I talked to Grace at several sales, and then she advised me it would be best if we were not seen talking together. I was not surprised, since the Freeport antique salesgoers had watched me take all the fine antiques in their area back to Dixon with me for some time, and did not have the kindest feelings toward me. I would meet with Grace an hour or so before sale time when few people were around.

It was hardly a month after we'd set up our pact that Grace told me of a lady in her town who had box after box of her grandmother's antique glass and china dishes that she wanted to sell, adding that she wanted a good price for them.

The thought of what might be in all those packed boxes wrapped up in 40-year-old newspapers made me very impatient. It would take only four or five good, signed art glass pieces to make this worthwhile. Grace had told me that when the boxes were unpacked, she would call me. She promised that while the dealing was going on, she would keep quiet, even though she was a good friend of the granddaughter who was doing the selling.

It occurred to me that this was a strange deal, with Grace making the friend her pigeon for a 10% finder's fee. I wondered why the friend had not called one of the Freeport dealers.

Grace and I finally got the date set for me to drive up--and it had to be alone--to meet her mysterious friend. I was to go, not to the friend's home, but to an apartment where the sale items would be displayed.

When I arrived at the address, it turned out to be an old two-story apartment house. I was to go to the back and up two flights of stairs. There an unsmiling Grace met me at the door, but winked through her round, gold-frame glasses. I was led into the dining room of a clean-appearing apartment and introduced to Arlene, whose last name I never learned.

Right away I could tell that Arlene was not going to be anybody's pigeon. She was around 50, with black, curly hair, and was a bit too heavy to be attractive to me, but she was not dumb by any means. I can always tell as soon as a few words are said. This is the way you get after you have bought and sold as much as I have.

Laid out before me in the dining room on a big ping pong table were hundreds of pieces of old glass and china, with a smattering of clocks on the floor.

Now began the longest bargaining session of my life. I soon found out that Arlene liked two other things about as well as her grandmother's dishes: cold cans of beer and cigarettes. As time passed in the hot apartment, I welcomed the beer myself as I struggled to keep my temper during the on-again, off-again dealing.

First Arlene asked for $3,000 for all the antiques. When I turned this down, she changed it to $1,000 for a small table full, then to $500 for only 10 items. One of these was a signed R. S. Prussia red-mark creamer and sugar with the rare lion on the sugar and his lioness on the creamer, worth, I figured, at least $750 for the pair. Then Arlene changed her mind again. She was going to sell me all her grandmother's dishes together, or none at all.

After six or seven beers apiece we had still not agreed on a price. Morning had worn into afternoon. Grace sat on a chair nearby, and as she had promised, did not interrupt the bargaining, except to tell Arlene several times that she thought I had offered her a good price.

Finally, I thought I would try again for a few of the best items. Pulling a small round table to the side of the ping pong table, I picked out several of the very best things. Of course I picked up the lion and lioness R. S. Prussia creamer and sugar, nonchalantly, so as not to arouse Arlene's suspicion. I offered $500 for the spread.

"No deal," said Arlene, only half sober.

I put the good stuff back on the table and bid for the last time. "Thirteen seventy-five for everything in the room but you."

Arlene agreed. By this time, over seven hours had passed, and both of us were about pie-eyed.

I sobered up fast when Arlene told me that all of her grandmother's **best** things were still boxed up, with one item being a big Tiffany lamp that was at least three feet tall and on a big tree trunk base. Arlene told me it had thousands of small leaded panels in shades of green and violet and was beautifully scalloped.

Instantly, I thought of the great Tiffany Wisteria, worth $45,000 for the small version and $100,000 for the bigger size, which this one was from the description! I asked Arlene when I could see the lamp and the other antiques.

"Get in touch with Grace, and she'll let you know," Arlene said. "I have to be away for two weeks now, so let's set up a time with Grace after that."

I was to go for one and a half years without being able to contact Arlene again, or find out where she lived or what name her phone was listed under. I called Grace dozens of times to try to pry Arlene's address and phone number out of her. She seemed to be afraid of telling me, because she said time after time, "I just can't tell you. She has had a lot of problems, and she's been sick," and on with other excuses to keep me away from the $100,000 Wisteria. No amount of bribe money that I could offer changed things. I even went to Freeport with a friend to quiz people all up and down the street near the apartment, but no one could tell me anything.

Then on one call, Grace told me that Arlene had unpacked the Wisteria, adding that it was "absolutely beautiful."

"It made my eyes blink just looking at it unlit," Grace said. "And when she lit it, the whole room came alive."

I told Grace to go and see if the lamp was signed in either of two places I told her to look. Grace said she had already looked for the Tiffany signature around the rim of the shade, but couldn't find anything.

I let the conversation terminate, thinking of the lion and lioness creamer and sugar that I was taking offers on. I had an offer of $1,200 from a Hollywood, California, collector. I was asking him $1,575. We

The Tiffany "Wisteria."

finally agreed, over a year after I had purchased the pieces, to the price of $1,400. That was $25 more than I had paid for everything.

Don't look to have this happen to you every day, because it has only happened to me once or twice in my lifetime. As for the lamp, the wind was now gone from my sails, since Grace couldn't find a signature. I stopped calling her.

Around two years after this episode, I read a newspaper notice of a sale that was going to be held about 20 miles out of Freeport, with a lot of rich-sounding antiques and a lamp listed on the sale bill. The strange thing was, no owner was listed. I decided it was an outside dealer's "sick stock" being unloaded, and thought I would not go.

But the sale bill caught my eye again on the day of the sale. The lamp listed was described as "1,000-panel floral lamp." This could mean a cheap repro that some city dealer was trying to stick an innocent buyer with. Furthermore, the location was in an out-of-the-way place, at a lodge on a lake. It was a fishy-sounding sale, to say the best for it. Yet something prompted me to go.

It was 12:30 and a half-hour past starting time when I finally found the lodge. I practically ran inside, bidding as I came in on some rare Heubach 12″ piano dolls. Five more rare signed Heubachs came up, and I bagged them all at a low price.

It was then that I spotted one of the most beautiful leaded lamps I had ever seen lying in a kind of metal holder, with its scalloped greenish shade exposed to my view, with what seemed to be 2,000 panels of glass. I looked down at a heavy object I'd hit my foot against, and saw it was an elegant, almost three-foot-tall metal vine-covered tree trunk base.

I hurriedly glanced up at the sale-goers then, to see who my serious competition might be. I saw that Don Haynes, a fine lamp dealer from Rockford, was seated in the first row wishing that I hadn't come in the door at the last minute, so he could have walked out with the lamp for practically nothing.

I know it's got to be signed Tiffany, I told myself. Before the bidding on it got started, I asked the auctioneer if he would please turn the leaded shade over so I could see if it might be signed inside the top rim. I'd read in my new Tiffany book that this was sometimes the case. The auctioneer replied that the whole upper section of the lamp was loose, and if he turned it over, the panels might cave in. This cooled me off. I don't like to repair things after I buy them.

Then my bidding fervor was further chilled. The auctioneer added that he and his staff had looked for a signature on the lamp before the sale, and couldn't find one.

Even so, I bid $500 to start the lamp, and as I guessed would happen, Haynes bid $600. Up to $1,400 we went in a hurry, until I detected a waver in his hand and voice. I knew this was the time to play "stick 'em." My last nod was a bid for $1,450, as I didn't want to close the door on Haynes with a flat $1,500. Then I pointed to myself as if in doubt and asked the auctioneer, "Am I in?"

"Dan's in," he replied, and with that, Haynes took the bait. He raised the bid to $1,500, and got himself a broken, Tiffany-TYPE lamp. If he made even a nickel on it after repairing it, I thought, he would be lucky.

I then proceeded to buy three beautiful, scalloped edge marble-topped Victorian tables and several fine china and glassware pieces. Then I bought three more tables, leaving a few for other buyers.

As I was going out of the building after the sale, a toy collector named Fred Murphy waved at me.

"Who did all these marble-topped tables belong to, Fred?" I asked. "I bought six of them myself."

"Don't you know?" asked Fred.

"Why, no. Did they have a big house, that they needed all these tables?"

"Just one for every room," Fred answered. "Didn't you know that all these antiques came out of a bawdy house that the Freeport cops closed down a month ago? The old grandmother who used to run the place for 60 years died, I hear, and turned it over to her granddaughter to run. The old gal was known all over Freeport in the 1920's to 1940's for collecting fine antiques."

Just then a voice said, "Hi, Dan," and I damned near collapsed to see sweet, shy, and two-years-older Grace Bennett look up into my eyes. I couldn't imagine what she was doing there.

"There were a lot of nice things at the sale today, don't you think?" Grace said. "They all belonged to Arlene."

Suddenly a number of things became clear. Grace was needling me for friend Arlene, who was peeved that I had not paid her more for her dishes. I will always think that if I had paid her a better price, I'd have been called back to buy all the really fine antiques that she sold 20 miles out of Freeport.

Now I knew why Arlene's name was not on the sale bill, and why the sale was located out of town. And now I knew that the great Tiffany Wisteria lying over there just had to be signed on the crown, where those farm auctioneers would not have looked.

I still doubt Grace's knowing the exact place to look for the L. C. Tiffany signature. I will always maintain that if I had been at the sale an hour earlier I could have had the monster leaded shade tipped up, and there I know I would have seen "L. C. Tiffany Furnaces, N. Y. C.," and the $100,000 lamp would have been mine.

To keep me smiling, I can always think that this wasn't true. Who knows for certain today but Don Haynes!

10

DID YOU SAY THAT
FIVE-LEGGED SIDEBOARD
I BOUGHT WAS WORTH $30,000

I met Bill Stambaugh at a livestock auction barn at Chana in 1955, as I was waiting in line to load some steer calves. At that time, I was a livestock dealer as well as a part-time antique dealer and bartender, in order to put food on the table for three hungry mouths and another on the way.

As I stood outside my two-ton stock truck, I started to talk with Bill about antiques. He took me to the cab of his truck and showed me a pair of wooden duck decoys he had just bought, also a big Bowie knife, plus some pocket knives by Case and Remington which he said he collected. He suggested that I be on the lookout for any early American furniture or dated coverlets that I could find, plus other things in the early American folk art line which were brand new to me, but a collecting priority with advanced collectors.

From that time until 1973, when we said hard things about each other's collections, our friendship kept growing, with me selling Bill some great rarities along the whole spectrum of antiques.

It started with my bringing whatever knives, duck decoys, and early dated coverlets, plus old furniture and old primitive oil paintings I had found, to Bill at any of the dozen auctions barns where we bought pigs. One time I brought a dozen old duck decoys that he paid me one heck of a big price for, handing me $15 extra for mint. He knew all there was to know about everything old. Where and how he acquired all his knowledge is still a mystery to me.

I made a lot of serious money being Bill's picker. It might be coverlets in reds and blues with eagles and White House decor dating from the 1840's, or rare folk art. The 1960's brought to light many fine period and folk art works of the early American wood worker, printer, and textile-maker.

One of my more exciting finds occurred in 1972 after I had driven to Rockford to a sale that promised very little, only several rare paperweights and a very old sideboard. It was just as I feared with the paper-weights, they were circa 1965. Ed Massey was one of the best auctioneers in the country, but he did sometimes misjudge the age of his glassware.

As I walked around the sale, which was held next door to a barbershop run by the owner of the sale goods, I nearly had a stroke when I saw standing, all dusty, one of the greatest early American Hepplewhite cherry sideboards ever to appear in the history of early American furniture. One of the six legs had been broken off about 10″ up, on a corner of the dainty sideboard's curved front.

When I walked closer, I began to see and understand why Bill had told me to keep my eyes peeled for pre-1800 American furniture, especially for the more beautiful city kinds, such as Hepplewhite of 1790, Chippendale of 1780-90, or an American Queen Anne piece, 1720-50, with its dainty pad feet. This piece of furniture was beautiful even in its damaged and dusty state. I looked harder at the satinwood inlay around the top, and then I fell back in admiration as I saw its small doors below, where an American eagle clutching arrows and surrounded by stars was beautifully inlaid into the cherry wood. The sideboard was a little over six feet wide with a slightly curved, semi-circular front.

Looking closely at the remaining legs, I saw that cornflowers were inlaid all the way down their slim, tapering surface. Above each leg was a big, inlaid star. I then knew I would have to buy this great Maryland or Massachusetts-made Hepplewhite sideboard at any cost, because even with a leg off, it was an important piece of early American city-type furniture, which was even in 1972 bringing record prices.

Then I saw a note in old, Spencerian handwriting attached to the top of the sideboard. As I began to read, I darned near fell over again. The writing told me this distinctive piece had been brought to the Midwest about 1850 by an ancestor of an important local family.

As the piece came up for bidding, I saw that my opponents were two early American dealers who had spotted the sideboard, and I was sure would make a determined effort to take it home. My chief rival was Jerry Finkle, known as the cheapest dealer in the country. There was a saying among dealers that if Jerry was bidding against you and you bought a piece away from him, you could count on doubling your money. Therefore when Jerry bid $310, I felt confident in bidding $320, which got me the piece.

As I was about to load the sideboard, the barber told me he had often loaned money for beer to the old man who owned it previously and kept it in his attic. The barber got tired of the $1 and $2 loans and made a deal to pay him $50 for the sideboard.

Looking back, I know that the piece should have stayed in Dixon or Grand Detour, connected as it was with an early family. But I thought that since it was missing a leg, I had better sell it to Bill, as he would know how to repair it. I am a guy who gets nervous, my wife says, if I hold anything over one day without peddling it, and she was oh! so right! in the case of the great 1790 Maryland cherry wood sideboard with inlaid eagles and stars and dainty cornflowers blooming down its beautiful, tapered legs.

I quickly called Bill up when I got home, wondering how much I should ask for the rarest piece of early American furniture and most superbly constructed I had ever found. I quickly described the sideboard, dwelling mainly on the two eagles inlaid in the small front doors. Bill asked me how much. I told him $700, and he tried to beat me down because of the missing front leg. That was late in the evening.

The next morning Bill was knocking at my porch door at 5 a.m. As I let him in, I thought I would scare him back home by naming a higher price of $750. He argued a minute, but when we walked down to the barn and he took just one look, he backed up his station wagon, paid me, and was gone.

Gone but not forgotten is the best way to describe my only chance to have become rich with one antique,

and I muffed it. The story that I had sold a signed Goddard sideboard for $750 made all the gossip among
good period furniture dealers at the Midwest antique
shows for some time to come.

Goddard, the greatest of all Hepplewhite and Chippendale city furniture makers, signed most of his
pieces somewhere. I didn't even bother to look until
we were loading the museum-piece, and there, as I
helped tip it up, I saw the Goddard signature. In one
fell swoop, I had lost most of $50,000.

When I looked at the sideboard as a guest in Bill's
house a year later, the leg had been replaced, and all
of its cornflowers were as exact as on the original
ones. Bill told me he had spent all that winter building
a leg to match as closely as possible so it could pass
as an original leg.

As I looked at the overall beauty of this great
triumph of Goddard woodworking skill, I could see
why the Stambaughs told me it was by far the most
outstanding piece in their collection, a collection that
had taken scores of years to build, and though housed
in an unpainted farm house, was easily worth $1
million.

It included early American folk art, Bowie knives,
over 50 fine Kentucky rifles, duck decoys by the country's best carvers, fine dated coverlets, red-painted
primitive furniture, a big room full of bisque dolls, two
or three sets of flow blue dishes, and many R. S.
Prussia scenic pieces. Still, Bill said once more, that
the Goddard sideboard was their finest piece.

It wasn't long after this that Bill came to my home,
and I thought I would try to work a compliment out
of him on my large and fine collection of Victorian
furniture. Bill told me Victorian furniture was too new

and nothing but junk to him.

I then told him, "All that barn-red, primitive furniture that you collect is nothing but junk to me too." Since he left that day in 1973, ten years have passed and we still don't talk.

A Goddard diminutive cherry sideboard with inlaid cornflowers and eagle.

11

THE FABULOUS
TWO GRAY HILLS
INDIAN RUG

It seems like an eternity ago that I first looked at and fell in love with an Indian rug. I was at a big flea market close to Chicago in 1963 when I got knocked off my pins by one that was hanging in a booth, and from that day to this, my torrid love affair with Indian rugs has not cooled. I am convinced that the Navajo weavers had to be touched by God to weave such masterpieces out of practically nothing.

At the time I saw my first Indian rug, I was heavy into orientals, so I had a natural love for all good rugs. As I stepped up closer to examine the weaving of the Indian rug, I realized it was as fine as that of the Kermans I had been selling.

When the dealer told me the rug was priced at $300, I was shocked. I bought an Indian rug price guide he was selling, and studied it for about a month before I inserted my ads to buy Indian rugs in several trade journals. Up until that time, I was known as mainly a paper goods dealer, so I expect observers of the antique scene thought it strange to read of Dan Shiaras wanting Indian rugs.

Soon letters and calls started to come in, and the beautiful Indian rugs with them. There were Yeis with their mythological figures in rows in browns, red, and blacks on a tan background. They were usually four to five feet long. I used to sell a five-footer for $800.

I soon got an over-supply of eye-dazzlers from four to nine feet in length. These were rugs with a lot of red in lightning-bolt patterns that sold big to tourists along reservation highways during the 20's and 30's.

The crystals had a white background with a few black and red bands crossing it. Often coarsely woven without much design, this rug was a poor-sell for me.

Occasionally someone would send me a chief's blanket or rug. A chief's rug is about six feet long with a design that meets in the center and is the same on both halves. A Chief's rug will over-power you with its beauty. I would sell a good mint one for $600.

A rug from eight to 10 feet in length is called a blanket. In the 1965 era, a blanket used to sell for $1,200 to $1,400 if it was in mint condition with a weave of 15 to 20 knots to the inch. The big galleries in the West refer to both rugs and blankets as Indian "weavings."

I used to advertise that I would pay $100 for a nice Indian rug. You can image the shock I'd get when someone would box up a valuable Yei or blanket eye-dazzler and send it to me for the $100 I was offering. The rugs I am describing were sold for $20 and $30 in the 1910-1940 era to tourists by the Navajos in New Mexico and Arizona. Squaws did the weaving on upright poles set in the ground. A six-foot rug would take three or four months to complete.

In early years the squaws used tree bark and berries to dye their rugs. This produced browns and grays, colors that did not sell well at that time. Then reds and other bright dyes were introduced from the East, and these colors caught on with the tourists. They would "dazzle" the eyes as the tourists drove through the reservations.

I always favored the eye-dazzler over all. I guess I am in the minority, because the customers to whom I sold 1,000 fine Indian rugs did not like them nearly as well as rugs of more subdued colors.

My rug buyers were centered mostly in Texas. The secret was to find a dealer or collector who had big money and could absorb 50 or 100 $600 rugs. This way I avoided expensive pictures in magazines. I simply sent the buyer a photo with a description as to condition, tightness of weave, and bleeding, if any, of dyes.

As the years went by, the prices I received for good Indian rugs started to escalate. The higher the prices went, the fewer good rugs I could locate with my nationwide advertising.

Towards the end of my Indian rug career, a man from Rockford, Illinois, called me in response to my ad in the town's paper, the first I had ever placed there for Indian rugs. The caller told me he had a very big Indian rug, he thought perhaps nine by 12 feet. He told me it was reddish in color and boldly designed, and had been appraised for $3,000 ten years before.

I got excited, because I began to think my caller might have a rare tribal rug, made by all the weavers in one part of the Navajo nation.

I drove up to see my caller, and he took me out to

his chicken shed. There on the ground was a worn-out American Sarouk machine-made rug.

I asked the Rockford man if he had any more "Indian" rugs, feeling it was useless to ask. He said he had some in his car trunk that he had just taken out of a bank vault, and he invited me into his house while he went to get them. I told myself that if they were really Indian rugs, he had probably taken them to an Indian rug buyer nearby for appraisal, and I might just as well forget about buying any Indian rugs from him.

He came into the living room carrying the rugs in a plastic bag. I doubted that I would really see any Indian rugs come out of his dusty plastic bag. He had to be nuts to call me to come and see the dirty American Sarouk. American Sarouks are made in factories by weaving machines, in imitation of the hand-made Sarouks that were woven in Iran from 1910 to 1940.

I stood and waited as my host began shaking the so-called Indian rugs out onto the living room floor. The biggest one, folded up, didn't even hit the floor before I knew it was a Two Gray Hills, and it was nearly blanket-size.

The Two Gray Hills rugs came from the region around Santa Fe where the best weavers in the Navajo nation were located in the 1920's. You get to know the great Indian rugs with just a glance. This rug was a blanket rug, over seven feet long, and woven in tones of brown and gray, which are always the colors of the Two Gray Hills rugs. It had a wide border all around of geometric figures that met in the center, and a beautiful tapestry weave of over 25 knots to the inch.

I spread the rug out a little more to see if it might be torn or spotted, and saw that it was in absolutely mint condition. All the while, I could feel every fiber in me tighten and my heart start to race faster and faster. I knew that before me lay the rarest Indian rug in the country. Was I going to be able to buy this rug, or was I going to go away without it?

Suddenly I knew what the seller was talking about when he had told me over the phone that the room-sized red "Indian" rug had been appraised for $3,000. He had gotten the old Sarouk in the chicken shed confused with this rug. The 7½′ by 5½′ black and tan rug at my feet had to be the one appraised for $3,000, and I knew it was worth triple that now.

I just barely looked at the other rugs. They were circa 1930 eye-dazzlers and crystals in four and five foot lengths and a six-foot saddle blanket, all in mint condition though 40 to 50 years old. Some of them still had clipped to them their original trading post tags. But most fabulous of all was the great Two Gray Hills rug that I was looking down at. I meant to buy those rugs just as a good boxer means to win a fight.

I started out by trying to get a price for the whole collection, but the seller would not name one. I hate it when people say they don't know what they want for their things. If you offer too low and they have anything heavy handy, they might hit you with it. Actually, people all know how much they want.

In this case, I found, the rugs did not belong to the man I was dealing with, but to his mother, who was 80 years old and ill in bed at her home. He didn't know anything about rugs, he said, so why didn't I make an offer?

I couldn't keep my eyes off the big black and gray, beautifully woven Two Gray Hills. If a three-footer in this type of rug, with its high-density tapestry weave similar to Iran's greatest hand-woven rugs, was selling for $3,500, as I knew it was, then this biggest Two Gray Hills ever to surface in the Midwest would retail for $10,000. There it was lying at my feet, and I was about to turn on every bit of buying power I had gathered in my long experinece to get it.

My opening bid was $600. The seller jeeringly answered that he would like to buy the rugs from his mother for that much himself.

You can scare off a prospective seller if you bid too high on an item as an opening offer. The seller will say to himself, if it is that good, I better get it appraised. You must play it cool, even though your heart is beating one thousands times a second like mine was that day.

Besides, said the Rockford man in turning down my opening bid, the big rug had been appraised for $3,000. I reminded him that he had told me over the phone that the red rug out in the shed was the one that had been appraised for $3,000.

We continued to talk for another 15 or 20 minutes, during which I learned that the seller's mother had brought the rugs back from the West in the 20's and had never put them on the floor, because she loved Indian rugs too much to see them walked on. I learned also that the seller worked in the downtown office of a large insurance company, while his wife was a bank teller.

I began to fear that my chances of buying the rugs were only 50-50, as it sounded as if the family did not need the money. However, guessing that by this time the Rockford man had a price in mind, I told him, "I'm not going to fool around on the rugs, so how about $1,000 for them, even though it's too much?"

This made his ears prick up. He said he would call

his wife at the bank. I was on pins and needles while he made the call. To my surprise, he came back with the word that his wife thought my offer should be accepted, but he would have to check with his mother.

I listened to him relay my bid and tell his mother it seemed like a good one to him and his wife, so what did she think? The mother told her 60-year-old son that she would never sell for that price. She'd just put the rugs away or give them to her friends.

Now if I jumped the bid too high, it would look like I had been trying to steal the rugs! However, I raised my offer to $1,350 for the queen of all post-1900 Indian rugs and her friends, each worth $200 at the time. There was roughly $11,000 worth of mint Indian rugs, I thought, lying there at my feet.

Once more the insurance man called his wife at the bank and again she encouraged him to sell the rugs, to pay his mother's doctor bills. Again he called his mother. I reflected that it was very difficult to buy anything in the antique line that had sentimental attachment, as these rugs seemed to have for his mother. However, the fact that they had been bought for next to nothing during the Depression was in my favor.

Mother told son that she had better keep the rugs. I could hear him parry her by saying, "But Mother, why keep them? He is going to pay you $1,350 for them."

At this point, I asked if I could speak to the mother myself. I asked her, "Isn't $1,500 enough for your rugs, M'am?"

"I thought you said $1,350?"

"I told your son to tell you (and I spoke loud and clear) that I'd pay you $1,650 for them."

Mother then said she wanted to speak to son

again. I heard him tell her that this seemed a fair offer and that she should take it. But it seemed that Mother was holding out for $1,850.

When I heard the son tell his mother that he would bring her the money as soon as he could, if I agreed, I knew I had at last landed the rarest and highest-value Two Gray Hills ever woven. I paid the $1,850 and quickly put the rugs back in the old plastic bag and exited the scene of the crime before any change of mind could occur.

I have always felt that antiques do people very little good when they are kept locked up and not enjoyed. I always figure they can do me a lot more good if I can buy them and use the profit to feed my family. Besides, many people who have antiques would rather sell them when they feel their time has come, and have the money to distribute evenly to relatives, than have a free-for-all over the antiques when they are gone. I have seen family members stop talking to one another permanently when a division is made of a loved one's antiques.

Once I got back home with the Two Gray Hills, I couldn't sit still until I got it appraised. I knew the person to do it, a professor and museum curator, and the greatest Indian artifact expert in the nation, to whom I had sold fine beadwork. When I phoned him, he told me to take a couple of good close-up photos and send them.

It was only a few days later that I received an excited call from the professor.

"Dan, your Two Gray Hills rug was woven by Rose Maloney, of the Gray Mountains," the professor said. "It was shown by her at the 1962 Arizona State Fair, and it walked away with a blue ribbon over all

The 5½′x7½′ Two Gray Hills Indian Rug.

other Southwest rugs. It is worth $10,000 average, and at a red-hot Indian rug auction the price could bounce to $12,500.''

I could hardly believe all this great news about my rug.

I decided to call, as well, a lady rug expert in Rockford. I told her I was a dealer whom a local bank had called in to do some appraising (a little white lie), and I needed help on some Indian rugs. I offered to pay her $100 to come to my house and look at them. The reason I sought this second appraisal is that I didn't want to end up looking foolish by putting an unrealistic price tag on the picture of the Two Gray Hills in my ad.

The appraiser turned out to be a lady in her 30's who had grown up in the family's Indian rug business. She looked at the Two Gray Hills very carefully, and then asked me if I would sell it. I explained I was just a go-between and it was not mine to sell. She admired the weave and added that the rug was the biggest Two Gray Hills she had ever seen. However, she pointed out a one inch round spot in light purple in the center of the rug, and told me that a Two Gray Hills should not have even a dot on it of any other color than browns, blacks and grays. But she said the spot might not seriously affect its value. She wrote down $8,500 as her appraisal.

"Really that much?" I said, delighted. She told me that the year before she had sold a three and one-half foot Two Gray Hills for $3,500.

On the basis of these appraisals I made up an ad picturing the rug and sent it to the **Antique Trader**. Expecting many calls to buy it for its $10,000 price, I stayed close to the phone. I didn't get even one call.

I knew right away something was wrong. I decided to write and see if the professor would buy the rug at a big discount from his appraisal. When I got no answer, I offered it to the lady appraiser for $6,000, telling her I had purchased the collection from the heirs. When I still got no answer, I knew that this greatest of all Navajo rugs was worth only what I could get for it.

I put the rug away for a few months, and then along in the fall, I told Fran to get the car set for a trip to New Mexico and Arizona to sell the rug. I had in the meantime sold the other rugs to a St. Louis collector. However, it was apparent to me that in a time lapse of ten years the Indian rug market had sagged, and it was all because there weren't the rugs around any more to make a market, as in the 60's when I was selling them like hot cakes.

So you see how it goes whenever you think your antique is the best. How proud you are of it! But when two or three professional appraisers turn it down, you then put thumbs down too on your antique, and tuck it away in some spot where you cannot be reminded of it. This is exactly the way I began to feel about the Two Gray Hills. I didn't wrap it up carefully any longer, and before we drove out the gate to Albuquerque, I just slung it into the back seat, all the while cursing the appraisers who had put a high price on it just to make me feel good.

I was sick from medication for a rare blood-chemical disease as we left town, but I am a very determined person. I took an extra pill and told Fran we would go from western state to western state and finally to Scottsdale, Arizona, where a big Indian rug and artifact auction is held monthly, until the rug was sold.

On the way we stopped at a western store in Oklahoma, where a gracious lady proprietor agreed to look at the rug for a friend who collected Indian rugs. She examined the Two Gray Hills with an experienced eye and said she thought her friend would like it. But after consulting with him, she came back with the verdict that the $6,000 price was too high, and he would pay no more than $3,500. I turned the offer down.

We finally reached Old Town in Albuquerque, where I went to the shop of a Jewish rug dealer who had been recommended. I asked him if he cared to take a look at a Two Gray Hills I had for sale. When he learned it was priced at $3,000, he told me that he bought Two Gray Hills rugs of my size for $1,200 every time he had an order for one. He said if he bought a high-priced rug like mine, he might have to wait six months or a year for a buyer. But he would show it to his wife. He came back saying they were not interested because of the small purple spot.

By this time I was not only sick physically, I was also sick of the rug. Fran took one look at me and announced we were heading for home. By the time we got as far as northern Texas, I told her to take us through the town where the western store was located to see if the proprietor would still be interested.

When we got there, I took the rug in and laid it out on the floor amid the oh's and ah's of clerks. When the proprietor came in, she took one look and smiled as she asked, "Is the price $3,500 now?" When I said yes, she smiled an even bigger smile and replied, "I have just the buyer for that beautiful rug." I was on the road to recovery.

The Two Gray Hills was my most memorable

Indian rug buy in the decade of the 60's , during which I probably bought and sold more good rugs than any other dealer outside the Southwest. If I had not been ill, I would have done what I set out to do and come close to selling the greatest rug on the market at that time for near its appraisal price.

At one time, scores of the better Indian rugs were sent to me each year. I used to pile them three feet high all around our living room for safe-keeping. Then I made all these rugs available to the nation's rug collectors at a minimal mark-up, during those 1960's years. My Indian rug customers were a special breed. They would much rather wear rags than pass up a good Indian rug, and it is still that way today.

Later, I advertised for Indian rugs nearly a year in all five of our biggest trade papers, and only a few were offered to me, so I quit looking. Once rug buyers found out that American Indian crafts were a better investment than money put in at interest, this slammed the door on Indian rug-selling as a business. I may run across a few rugs every year, but not like the days when the eye-dazzlers, Yeis, and chief's rugs used to lie in big piles around my house. I shot down over 1,000 of them in the 60s, and while it lasted, it was great sport.

Let me sum up what to look for if you decide to buy an Indian rug:

1. Be sure to buy one at least five feet long.

2. Be sure the rug is clean and blemish-free. Moths have a great fondness for Indians rugs.

3. Be sure the rug doesn't look "bled." A bled rug is one in which the colors have run. If an Indian rug is washed with soap and water, the vegetable dyes will

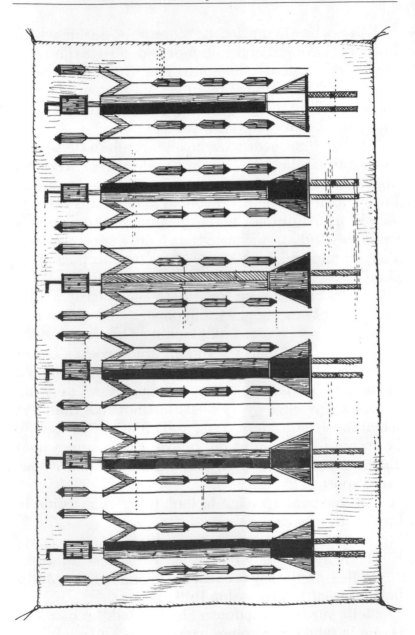

A Yei, 4′ x 6′, $800-$1,200.

usually run, causing a $600 rug with beautiful reds and tan to run into the whites. Price on a bled rug will go down to $75 or even $50. I have tried on occasion to have dirty rugs cleaned with no better results. The analine dyes used after 1920 can withstand washing or dry cleaning better than those in the earlier rugs.

4. Count the knots along one inch of your pocket ruler. If less than 20, I would advise you not to invest in the rug. The higher the weave, the better the rug.

5. Hold the back of the rug up in front of you and see if you can see the diagonal lines like scars where the weaver joined on new pieces of yarn. These are called "lazy lines." If you cannot see the lazy lines, the rug may be a hand-loomed but inferior Mexican rug that can fool a new buyer and lose him a lot of money. Many Indian rugs also have three strands of 3"-long wool protruding from their corners. These are the "evil spirit lines" that let evil spirits escape from the rug.

6. Try to get a written statement from the seller as to the rug's approximate age. If it is later than 1940, don't buy.

7. Buy a rug only if it "speaks" to you. If it speaks to you and you must have it, then it will also appeal to potential customers if you decide to sell it.

Today Indian craft transactions are breaking old record prices. An Apache circa 1888 coil weave basket recently sold for $30,000 at the Sotheby Galleries in New York. Indian crafts are one of the best things to invest your extra money in today. Happy hunting. The Indian was a great artist, but many of us found out about it too late for cheap buying.

Post Cards Ring The Cash Drawer Bell

High priced postcards: Santa, $8.50; Halloween, $8; German natural hair postcard, $12.50; Kewpie, $30; Sun Bonnet Baby, $12.50; Sleepy Eye Flour, $65; Cracker Jack bears, $20. All about 1910.

12

POST CARDS--THE SLEEPER
THAT'S RINGING THE
CASH DRAWER BELL

What do you suppose is the surprising best buy in the collecting field today--something that you can invest $100 in and expect it to pay off when the times comes to cash in on a lifetime's collecting fun?

The fastest-growing and potentially most profitable hobby today, in my opinion, is collecting pre-1920, and preferably the pre-1915, postcards. The two largest stamp and coin publications, *Lynn's Stamp Weekly* and *Coin World Weekly*, came out recently with special postcard classified sections. An article in one of them concurred with my opinion that good old postcards are a blue ribbon investment, and both stated their intention of carrying postcard articles and buy and sell ads.

I became interested in postcard collecting in 1962 when I was peddling one of the antique dry sinks I occasionally found to Vergie Swan, a dealer in Grand Detour. She was an old gal with a lot of antique savvy whose shop was always full of a big variety of pattern glass, primitives, dolls, and good old pine furniture plus brass and copper articles in her stone barn next door. Her prices were atrociously high in my opinion, but she must have been getting them, because every Saturday night about 6 p.m. I could watch her walk into the Dixon National Bank carrying a big pocketbook at the end of a leather strap which looked overloaded with money from that week's take.

At that time I was barely making it, with a wife and four children to feed. I stopped at her shop one day with a nice small dry sink in my truck, and caught her sorting post cards. When I told her I had found her another good dry sink, she looked up just long enough to say, "How much?" She always looked at me over the top of her gold spectacles like a district attorney does a murderer when questioning his testimony. It kind of scared me into reducing the prices of the things I brought her.

"How does $5 sound?" I asked Vergie.

"Make it $3 and drop it off over at the barn. That's the best I can do," she said.

Since there wasn't anybody else buying dry sinks that I knew of in those days, I agreed. When I went in to get paid, I began to watch Vergie slowly going through what looked to be all the old postcards ever made. I asked Vergie how many postcards she had to organize, thinking she was a bit daft to be sorting what appeared to be over 50 cartons full. She said she had bought a collection of 100,000 cards from a dealer. Being nosy as usual, I asked her what the cards cost. She kept sorting as she said, "Two cents each."

This was all the information I needed to get started on having, during the next 15 years, one of the best times I was ever to have in the antique business.

At first I used to buy postcard albums for a few dollars, and cream the best cards, such as Santa Clauses, Kewpies, Sunbonnets, ships, trains, and Halloween scenes, for myself; and then fill in the empty album spaces with average cards. I must admit, ashamedly, that I used to sell these creamed albums through national ads. Postcards by then had caught on and I could easily get $25 to $30 for a 300-card album. Now a similar album can cost $300 at an auction. I used to get some hurrahs for albums sent to customers, but an equal number raised Cain with me when they could not find even one good card such as a Santa Claus in the album I had sent them.

In the meantime, I was becoming possibly the biggest card collector in the area, with 20,000 of all great cards. Over the years I kept throwing my good cards into a couple of 10-gallon tin cans with lids, that stood in an unused room in our house. While I never completely filled them, I did come close to filling one of them by the time I quit collecting in 1974.

By 1978, postcards had blown their price lid off at the post card auction markets, with Old Sleepy Eye cards from the Sleepy Eye Flour Mill Co. at Sleepy Eye, Minnesota, leading the way at the Chicago auction at $75 each, and card after card selling from $10 to $25. I then decided I had better buy some albums with plastic card holders and begin filling each one up with categories like Santas with full suits, Santas with half-suits (that sold then for $5 each), brown-suited Santas, $20, and rare purple, green and black-suited Santas, up to $50 each. Then came the Rose

O'Neill Kewpie cards at $20 each.

There were albums filled with Cracker Jack bears at $20 each. I had a complete set of 16 Teddy Roosevelt bear cards, worth around $500. Then there were busy bears, sea-shore bears, and silk and satin appliqued bears. I favored bear cards over all in those days.

Next, I had hundreds of comical postcards showing Blacks, which are currently selling as high as $20 each at Chicago-area flea markets. All of my good Halloween, Thanksgiving, Fourth of July, Lincoln, Washington, and flag, ship, and steamboat cards were put in my albums in sections, most of them worth $2 a card. Then there was a gob of advertising cards. By the time I was done putting my cards into the albums, I had filled almost 70 albums of 300 cards each, totalling about 20,000 cards. There was a small fortune in cards sitting in that unused west room in our old farmhouse in 1978.

Then while we were gone to Disneyworld, some person or persons broke the door lock to that room and stole all my cards. To say that I was sick, is not saying half enough. Not only did 15 years of saving the best cards go down the drain, but at $2 a card, $40,000.

From the two cents and three cents I'd get for good cards in 1963, it is a far cry to the $2 up to $75 that good pre-1920 card will bring today. As for the prognostication of the post card future, all say they will double and triple in price in just a few years. Many postcards are small works of German art that for their striking color and beauty will never be duplicated again.

Happy postcard hunting, everybody, but keep your cards in a vault and not in 10-gallon lard cans!

13

MAKING FIFTY YEARS'
EXPERIENCE PAY OFF
AT AUCTIONS

Before I start for a sale with Fran, my wheel man for 35 years, I make sure that my antique price guides are in the car, along with an up-to-date blue book on the latest doll prices, and any other book I think I might need in the battle to come with flea marketeers, antique show dealers, and collectors. A reference library of books on antiques is very important to the dealer, and price guides carried in the car may make him thousands.

Now that my answer phones are all set to take incoming messages regarding my latest national ads, Fran and I take off for the sale that I have picked as the most promising that day after reading sales bills in the several northern Illinois newspapers and five national trade papers that I subscribe to.

Fran loves every bit of the hunt for antiques. She is

even more gung-ho to go to a good sale than I am at times. It doesn't matter to her if the sale is 10 or 100 miles away.

Our yearly sales-going racks up 30,000 to 35,000 miles on our car. On the way to a sale, I relax and sleep to prepare for six to seven hours of standing on my feet in all kinds of weather. Sometimes I have cooked in 105 degree heat, and at other times have frozen at farm sales where cows and machinery are being sold along with the antiques in zero weather.

When we get to the sale, Fran helps me by looking over the antique china and glass, and especially the dolls, for even the smallest chips and hairline cracks that knock an antique's price down sharply at resale time. She also hunts through all the boxes for hidden sleepers that the farm auctioneers might have dumped into them, and which could make us some money. Once the sale commences, I do not keep the price guides with me. Never do you see a top-flight dealer consulting a price guide in public.

Fran also keeps me informed as to who is bidding against me. She may advise me to change seats or change my standing position so as not to be observed by certain parties.

Sometimes at an auction, other bidders will figure that if I am bidding, the antique must be good, and that I will bid only to where I can sell it at a good profit. Therefore they are determined not to stop until after I do, and this procedure can carry me into a big retail loss. It can also carry them into a fatal mistake.

I make mistakes as a buyer, too. Not many, but I make them, and for this, Fran gets madder than a hornet. She is a gal who was brought up on a small farm and was taught the value of a dollar. She says she was not born with a silver spoon in her mouth as she says I was (which is not true.) Occasionally I do deserve a good wife-lecture for my buys. It helps me to be a more careful bidder.

From time to time during the sale, out of the corner of my eye, I can see Fran sitting and visiting with various ladies. She will be saying over and over again who we are and where we are from.

At lulls in the bidding, I am asked a dozen or more times if I am in the antique business. An older man, seeing that I have just bought a set of Haviland, offers to sell me five sets and will bring them to me next week. A lady approaches me about a set of Haviland plus several old mint quilts that she will call me about

Alfred Meakin ironstone china in 1880s Tea Leaf pattern.
Cup and saucer, $55-$65.

selling. One more lady has a house full of fine antiques and a collection of 1840 French blown-glass Baccarat paperweights to sell.

So there is a lot of extra-curricular profit to be made at sales if you are a high-powered bidder.

Eating barbeques washed down with lots of fresh-made coffee from the lunch stands is also a fun part of auctions. At each sale, the barbeques are different and defy one to describe. Tables creak with home-made pies. I often take one home when I hit a fine flavor.

Fran boxes up all the antiques I buy and hauls them to our stationwagon, often a block away. She always pays the bill at the end of the sale, sometimes having to line up for half an hour. Once she has paid, she checks off everything I've bought from the list she was given, to be sure it is in the wagon. We usually leave with it loaded to the gills, and Fran still at the wheel, taking off for a nice place to eat if we are out of town. This is often the case with the three or more sales we go to each week.

For most of the 35 years of our married life, this is the way we have operated. It all began in 1948 as the orchestra played "I'm Going to Take a Sentimental Journey" and I danced with the prettiest girl in the dance hall while others kept cutting in.

For Fran the sales are a chance to acquire anything that she wants to keep for our home. When she likes something, it never fails to be superior. She has inborn good taste. Her favorite collectible is 1840 Chinese Rose Medallion china, and she has currently a super-fine collection of this colorful ware.

After a sale, Fran continues to scan all of the ten or so newspapers we subscribe to for announcements

Graniteware - a surprise sleeper. Thresherman's coffee pot in gray, $20-$25; blue, $75-$85; red, $150-$175.

of more good sales. She tacks these on the kitchen wall, and I read them all and select the sales I will go to that week. She then passes the rest of the week packing up all the antiques I have sold through my ads to take to UPS and ship.

Fran will not try to sell over the phone, as it is my job, she tells me. I do the buying and selling and she does all the rest. So who does the most work in our business?

14

HOW I CAPTURED THE
WELLER ART POTTERY
INDIAN CHIEF

Before I knew what Rookwood art pottery was, back in 1964, I bought a vellum scenic vase at a house sale in Dixon, with two lady antique dealers bidding against me. I paid $15 for the vase decorated with sailing ships, a big price in those days.

Art pottery, which has a painted floral, scenic, or other decoration under the glaze, was produced by about a dozen companies near the turn of the century. Rookwood and Weller were two of the major ones.

After paying so much for the piece of Rookwood pottery, I got nervous and put it in my cattle truck cab, hoping to sell it to a Princeton dealer whom I often stopped to see after cattle sales.

"Honest" John Barrow was what he was called, but he did not win that title because of his honesty. Formerly he had plucked chickens for a poultry dealer for a living, but he had quit that and turned to plucking pigeons in the antique game.

When I stopped to see John after the next cattle sale, he took one look at my rare vellum Rookwood vase, and when I asked him double what I paid for it, he immediately bought it.

Just one day afterward I read an article in a trade magazine describing how valuable Rookwood was, with a price tag of hundreds of dollars in its area of origin around Cincinnati. I nearly choked when I read this. It was one day too late.

I called Honest John and told him a desperate story. I said the lady who had sold the vase was in trouble at home for selling it, and would give $50 to get it back, and had asked me to try to get it for her.

"I broke it right after you left, Dan," Honest John said. "It slipped out of my hands and shattered in a thousand pieces. Sorry." John hung up.

He was not about to sell me back for $50 a great pottery rarity that he could sell elsewhere for $500.

A little later in my art pottery collecting days I spotted a book about Rookwood art pottery written by Joe and Barbara Agranoff. It told all about vellum glaze, which has a soft, cracked look, standard glaze, iris glaze, which is high-gloss and light colored, and matte finish glaze on Rookwood pottery, but gave no prices. I said to myself, I have five Rookwood standard glaze ewers, so why not give them a flyer in my next *Antique Trader* ad at five for $100.

The first to call was Joe Agranoff. I sold all five to him. It wasn't over six months later that a price guide came out giving each hand-decorated and signed floral cruet a price tag of $100 each. I was sick, because it had taken me several years of scrounging to collect the five.

The Rookwood Pottery was founded in 1880 in Cincinnati, Ohio, by Mrs. Maria Longsworth Storer. She named the factory after the family estate, which had a large number of crows around it. Mrs. Storer gathered together the finest chemists, potters, and artists during the period 1890-1925, and Rookwood quickly became the foremost art pottery in the world. When it received a gold medal at the Paris Exposition of 1889, the world became aware of it.

Rookwood artists, of whom scores were employed in the peak year of 1910, signed their names on the base of pottery pieces with initials only. Artist-signed pottery is worth several times more than the more common, unsigned pieces.

Rookwood pottery pieces were dated from the time the first reverse R was impressed in 1886. After this year, one flame was added each year to the top part of the R; by 1900, 14 flames adorned it. After 1900, a small Roman numeral beginning with I was placed at the base of the R and the flames discontinued.

Many of the companies that made art pottery continued to do so until the Depression closed them up. Rookwood continued production until 1941. Another great pottery company, Weller, produced its wares in Zanesville, Ohio, from 1873 to 1948. Rookwood and Weller vases that are signed by the artist have both been selling at big Eastern auctions at prices such as $5,000 for a Rookwood scenic vellum vase and $30,000 for an early Rookwood Indian chief.

I have owned some great pieces of art pottery, including a signed Sicard Weller 42″, two-part jardiniere that glistened like dark carnival glass, and which I bought at a Rockford auction early in the 70's for $15.

In 1975 I sold it to an Iranian rug dealer for $2,000.

So you see that you don't have to spend a lot of money to buy great art pottery if it has come out of the attic unrecognized or isn't advertised at a sale.

The first time I ever saw a piece of **Indian** art pottery was in Rockford in 1975. Bert Nichols, who works with the Roy Stenzel auction firm, came up out of a basement carrying the pottery piece in his arms like it was a big chunk of wood. Nate, my side-kick, and I did double-takes as we walked over for a closer look at the 31″ by 11″ umbrella stand, which we saw had a painting on the front of it of a war-bonneted Indian chief with war paint on his cheeks and a beaded shirt. The piece was done in standard high-glaze in browns, with the chief absoluely life-like in his skin tones.

What an art pottery painting, I told myself, and better yet, what a piece of early Weller! I told Nate to stand in front of it.

About this time, who should walk onto the sale grounds and start to snoop around as usual but Harriet "Flintface" Frazer, our old Stillman Valley nemesis. Whenever it came to anything Indian, Flintface would go just plain ape and throw her purse full of money at the auctioneer.

When I saw Flintface, I told Nate I would stand in front of the Chief, which I had turned around to face away from inquiring eyes. I knew Flintface would not come near while I stood watch, due to my sending her away crying in Lake Geneva from a hayrack of old magazines, and snookering her out of two dry sinks at Lena.

For half an hour I stood guard over the greatest piece of Weller art pottery ever seen in the Midwest. When the auction progressed to the point where the

The Weller Indian Chief, 31″x11″, $8,000-$10,000. Collection of William Trusz, Manchester, Mo.

Indian chief was to be sold, I jumped out and stood in front of Bert Nichols, and Nate again stood in front of the umbrella stand, concealing it from Flintface's piercing view. The bidding started out slowly on the umbrella stand, because few had seen it. One young couple ran it up to $200. Flintface kept turning her head and craning her neck to see exactly what was being sold, but she was never able to see because I as directly in her way.

Then some of the bidders asked for a better look. Since Nate was standing nearest it, Bert asked him to hold it up. As he did so, Nate showed Bert only the all-brown backside. With this, Bert was satisfied that the crowd had seen all they needed to. When I quickly ran the bidding up to $275, Bert cried, "Sold."

Flintface tried her best to see what had been sold in the pottery line for $275, but never did get a good look. Nate picked the chief up and ran as fast as he could through the crowd to lay the great piece of Weller art pottery in my car. He came back and told me we'd done a heck of a job in concealing from Flintface what was her meat.

I thought it was the happiest day of my life when I put the Chief down next to my fireplace and looked at him for awhile. That's the way it's been with thousands of beautiful art objects I have owned. I keep them for a short time and then share their beauty with my customers. So it was with the chief. A Missouri customer drove 600 miles non-stop to Grand Detour and smilingly took his prize back home.

15

MR. SHIARAS, DID YOU SAY
SOMEONE HANDED YOU A
FREE TIFFANY DAFFODIL LAMP?

In the summer of 1972 when I was into Mettlach steins big, word got to me that a party in Clinton, Iowa had a big Mettlach stein collection to sell, but my informant did not remember the name. The Clinton lady was supposed to have a house full of every other thing in the antique line, so this made me almost frantic to locate her and get her rare Mettlachs bought before they were eaten up by all the antique wolves along the Mississippi River whom I had bumped into at sales. If you ever bought anything from an Iowa dealer for resale, you would have to keep it for ten years until inflation raised its price.

To locate the unknown seller, I decided to run a blind ad in the Clinton paper saying that I bought old beer steins, and listing a box number. Unbelieveably, I hooked my fish with the first three-day ad.

From the sound of the letter I received, the Clinton lady still had the steins. I called her and she sounded like a big, friendly old gal. When we got to her address the next day, we found that was exactly what she was.

Fran stayed in the car as I went up to the door of a first-floor apartment. She was brought up never to go where she wasn't invited, but I'm different. I would go through a swarm of hornets just to get into a house that looked loaded with antiques. I envisioned a long row of five and six-liter Mettlach steins inside this apartment, just waiting for me to haul them home.

The plump, 60ish gal who greeted me with a broad smile looked past me and noticed Fran sitting in our car, and quickly motioned for her to come in. We entered a five-room apartment full of nice old things. It was hard to tell at once if there was anything good there because of the cramped quarters. As soon as I got adjusted to the dim light, I asked Mrs. Leamon if I could see her stein collection. She said I was just a day too late, as she had sold them all to a Des Moines antique dealer the day before. She said all that was left of them were on a ledge, and pointed to six or seven.

I walked over, and to my dismay saw only some ordinary German pottery steins that I could hardly sell for $75 each, and two three-liter common printed-under-glaze Mettlach steins that I could retail for $125 each. Nobody in the stein world that I sold to would give anything for a Mettlach printed-design stein or transfer type that was mass-produced by machine, and not etched and handpainted, such as the ones I sold for $300 for a half-liter.

From where I stood I threw out a low bid of $250. Mrs. Leamon thought over my price for a moment, and said, "Go ahead and take them, I don't have any use for them. Dad had a lot of them over at our big house across the street, but when he and Mother died a few years ago, I couldn't stand it over there. I never spent one happy moment there."

She pointed out the window to a beautiful, three-story stone mansion as being her old home. I then knew there had to be some really good stuff in her apartment, so I asked her if I could look around.

Alberta, as she'd told us to call her, gave me permission, and in the meantime with a tug of a cupboard door, brought into view a bar, and asked us to join her in a drink of anything in the house. I settled for White Horse scotch, and Fran had a glass of wine. It turned out that White Horse was Alberta's favorite drink, too. But I could see after just a few drinks that I couldn't keep up with her. While she kept punishing the scotch, I got up and looked around the cramped apartment. Fran, as I had taught her to do when we bought out of a house, packed up the steins I had bought and put them in the car. My policy is to get whatever you buy out fast before minds are changed.

As I walked from room to room, I nearly choked to see what I recognized even 20 feet away and standing on a table, as a big Tiffany lamp, with what seemed to be thousands of panes of leaded glass. The lower part of the shade was circled with bent yellow daffodils against a green background. I walked over to look for the Tiffany signature on the shade, and after a minute, I found it inside the shade along the rim where it is always supposed to be.

Then I happened to glance up to a shelf high above

A Free Tiffany Daffodil Lamp?

The Daffodil Lamp, $20,000-$30,000.

me, where I saw two art glass vases, swirled in leaf patterns in gorgeous reds and blues. Since Alberta didn't seem to give a hoot what I looked at, I stood on a chair, and when I lifted the vases to check for a signature, I found they, too, were signed Tiffany.

I then made up my mind I'd have to buy these, too, to take home with me. I suddenly remembered that we hadn't brought along enough cash to pay for an expensive Tiffany lamp and the signed Tiffany vases. This was more rare Tiffany than most dealers get to see in two lifetimes. I'd try to pay with a check, hoping Alberta would accept it from practically a stranger.

I sat down at the big table with Alberta, and she began to tell me about herself. Her father, a civil engineer, had drawn the plans for the locks in the Mississippi River, and had been a very wealthy man. She had lived with her parents in a brick and stone mansion across the street, with servants and all else that a main-line family had in those days.

Just a few months before Alberta had given away her dad's gun collection because she was afraid of guns. It had gone to a Texas gun dealer who had come up to buy them. There was a cased pair of gold-handled Hickock pistols in the collection, she said. I knew that this pair of guns alone would have sold for $10,000 at the time. Alberta had also given away her family's cut glass to a few friends, she told us, because she hated the sight of it after being forced as a girl to wash it every week instead of playing outside with other girls. She went on about her unhappy life with her parents in the mansion across the street, continuing to drink and putting her handkerchief to her eyes.

It was time to talk about my chances of buying the

gorgeous Tiffany in the next room before any more liquor was consumed.

I said, "Alberta, how much will you take for the old lamp in the other room?"

"Oh, go ahead and take it, Dan, I don't use it," Alberta said.

I almost fell flat backwards. I told Fran, after I had partially recovered, to go out and get a big box. After Fran had packed it, I carried it out to the car, slowly at first, but breaking into a fast trot as I travelled the last 20 feet. I quickly unlocked the car trunk and gently set down the big leaded Tiffany shade. I ran to get the base. Then I asked Alberta about the two vases on the ledge in the living room. I got my second shock of the day when with her handkerchief to her eyes, Albert told me to take them. She didn't want them around, she said.

I put the vases in a small box I had brought in, and at that point began to feel we had better leave before a sudden change of mind occurred.

But Alberta insisted she wanted to show Fran some of her mother's gold jewelry before we left. The main part of it was at the bank in a lock box. But she brought out a beautiful pink baroque gold ring set with ten Mississippi River pearls. She related how her father had drawn the plans for the locks on the river and as a thank-you, the government had given his wife the Tiffany-mounted ring. She told Fran to try it on her finger, and after she did so, told her, "It looks better on your finger than it did on Mother's. I want you to have it."

As soon as I could, I signalled to Fran with my eyes that we should leave. I wondered as we drove out of town if Alberta would call the Clinton cops to stop us as we drove off with all the free loot. I figured there was an easy $10,000 in the lamp, and $1,000 in the Tiffany vases and ring.

I soon advertised the Tiffany lamp and sold it to a big antique dealer in Seattle for good money.

We learned later than Alberta, who had no children, had begun to make short work of the contents of the big mansion soon after her husband died. Within two years she had sold the mansion itself. We made second, third, and fourth trips to visit this grand old gal who would rather give away her priceless antiques than sell them. But you had to be able to drink scotch with her drink for drink. I prided myself, at the time this story took place, on being a guy who could drink 12 or 13 martinis and still be half-way sober. Poor Fran, who can get pie-eyed on just one drink, used to pass out on me on the couch.

Here was a wonderful, 60-year-old lady whose bitter childhood - spent alone in a big mansion - had turned her against all that reminded her of those hateful days, and had given those bad memories away to the first people who came to her house. I got there just a few days too late for the $2,000 Mettlach steins and the rare gun collection. But I did get there in time for the daffodil lamp! It was the strangest antique call I ever made. Hate is a powerful force of evil, and it proved itself so again in this true story. When, in all the annals of antique collecting, will someone be given a signed Tiffany lamp again?

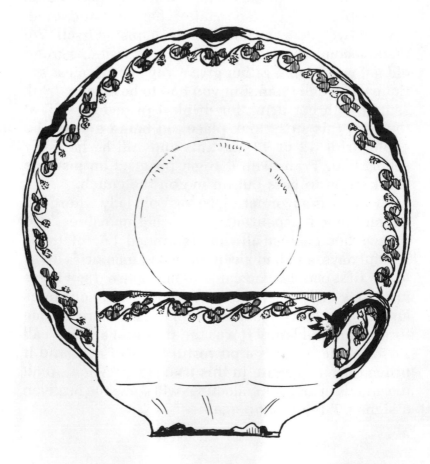

"Clover", one of the most popular Haviland patterns at $1,800-$2,000 for service for 12.

16

HAVILAND! A BEAUTIFUL NAME FOR A BEAUTIFUL DISH

The moment I laid eyes on my first set of French Haviland dishes at an auction in 1960, I liked this china. I had often heard the name bandied about as housewives got together, but I never quite knew what they were so excited about.

The first set I saw in the flesh was an all-white set with daintily scalloped gold edges, which is known as Schleiger #24. I looked hard at that set of china, and I determined there and then, if anyone bought it away from me, I would quit the antique business.

The set consisted of 12 dinner plates, 12 luncheons, 12 bread and butters, 12 soups (which are two-handled cups), 12 butter pats, 12 sauces, 12 tea-size cups and saucers, 12 coffee cups and saucers, 12 demitasse chocolate cups, 12 egg cups, a covered butter, sugar and creamer, gravy, waste bowl, an open vegetable, a round covered vegetable dish, two oblong covered vegetables, coffee pot, tea pot, and two relish dishes. Although it has been over 20 years since I saw this magnificent set, I recall it easily. This is what Haviland does to you. It will make you want to buy it whether you can afford it or not.

I was a married man with four children at the time I ran into this set at a private sale of the effects of a restaurant-chain owner. The price being asked for the Haviland set was unbelieveably high for those days, $450 for the over 144 mint dishes. I couldn't afford them at this high price, but still, I could make myself afford them, I thought, by selling a lot of my collectible glassware to other dealers. I took a chance, and without having enough money to buy food the next day, I wrote out a check.

There wasn't a flake or a crack on even one piece, as I examined the set and packed it. The estate's heir told me that her sister had collected the set over a long period. She would go into Marshall Field's in Chicago periodically in the old days, and bring back, first the set of 12 dinner plates. Then at another time she bought a few coffee cups, which are a bit larger than the tea size. It took her 20 years to complete the set, and then she kept it stored away in a high kitchen cupboard and never used it even for one dinner. When she passed away, the Haviland was still in the cupboard above the kitchen sink, and it remained there until I reached up and brought it down.

Today this set of Haviland with a double mark would be worth around $2,500, being ranked among Haviland's ten best all-time sellers, with Clover and Silver Anniversary considered by many to be in a tie for the Number 1 spot. My wife has a complete 144-set of Clover, and she would turn you down if you offered her a small fortune for it. She, too, is a Haviland addict.

Whenever you go to a sale and see a set of Haviland, be sure it is marked "Haviland" in both green and red on the back of each dish. The green mark alone on a Haviland set means it was not decorated at the Haviland factories in Limoges, France. It came to this country in an all-white set of dishes. This all-white pattern is called Schleiger No. 1, or Ranson. It was produced for a long time in France, and shipped to the States in the early 1900's for around $12 for a 144-piece set. When you see the double stamp on the back of a dish, it means all the dainty decorations of flowers, etc., were hand painted at the factory.

In a set of Haviland today, it is more important to have tea cups than the larger-size coffee cups. The two-handled ramekins, or soups, are not much in demand.

I have bought and sold scores of different sets of Haviland over the years, and have made very good money on all the sets. I used to sell whole or partial sets to Marie Baker's Old Toll Gate Antiques in Milan, Illinois, and to the Wagon Wheel Antiques, East Moline, Illinois. Both these shops are known around the country for being able to replace anything you might need in your set. They are known as Haviland hospitals, and the owners are in the national mail order business, just as I am.

Aids in identifying Haviland are Arlene Schleiger's six books, *Patterns of Haviland*, which designate over 800 sets. The job of locating your Haviland number may be either long or short. It is pure luck if you consult Schleiger's line drawings and find your pattern immediately. I have many times taken two or three hours to identify a pattern. But once I have it identified, I will put this information in my ad, and a potential Haviland customer will know exactly what I have and call me up to buy it.

In the 1960's and up to about 1976, French chefs in this country would buy all the Haviland sets they could get and export them back to relatives living in France, who in turn would spot them in small out-of-the-way Paris antique shops and wait for rich American tourists to see them. Thinking they were discovering a rare Haviland set, they would fork out double and triple the top retail price. French chefs got away with this for a long time. It was only the near-disappearance of Haviland on the U.S. market that made these crooks turn straight.

Haviland today is selling high. An 84-piece, 12-place setting of Clover sells quickly for $2,000; Ranson No. 1, $800; Drop Rose, $2,000; Silver Anniversary, $1,200; and the beautiful Autumn Leaf, $1,400.

If you break a cup belonging to your Haviland set, the replacement price from one of the big Haviland hospitals is around $30. If your set is one of the top ten best-sellers, the price may go as high as $60.

You see, girls, you must not be nervous when you observe old people with hands that tremble drinking tea from your valuable Haviland, or you well may shake so hard that you drop and break your own cup.

Haviland today is not so popular as it was 50 years ago or even 10 years ago, because fewer people are serving formal dinners. Haviland today is a status symbol, and it is fun to show off when friends drop in.

If you see "Theodore Haviland" on the back of a plate, it means the piece is a later Haviland, circa 1900.

It is usually not worth as much as the earlier, double-stamped Haviland. The painting is never as nice. If you see "Haviland, New York State" on the back of a plate, it means the plate was made in New York from 1937 to 1950 during the War years. Haviland simply moved much of its business of making dishes over here. This ware is as high priced, or even higher, than the old, delicate Haviland. I love to see New York State heavy, and to my notion, ugly, Haviland at a sale. It means, nine times out of ten, that I will buy it cheap and sell it high.

Do not become a Haviland dealer thinking you will make a lot of money. All you will do is what I have done all my years as a nationwide dealer, and that is make a darn good living. The days of making a fast buck are over, the collectors having access to reams of information on antique prices including prices on all the Haviland sets ever made.

The sets of double-mark Haviland which I have purchased over the years I, as a rule, bought for under $100 in the early days, and sent to a New York buyer to be sold many times for a 500% mark-up. Today I am paying up to $900 for all fine sets of double-mark Haviland with service for 12.

In buying a set of Haviland, do not buy one with chips or hairline cracks; be certain all the tea cups are there and not big coffee cups, alone; and be sure all the pieces of a fine set of dishes are present, because one missing butter dish costs $75 and up to replace. It is best to buy only the older Haviland with the double mark of "Haviland, France" in green, and "Haviland & Co., Limoges" in red.

I wish you as much pleasure with Haviland as I have had down through the years.

Royal Doulton Red-Haired Clown toby, $5,500.

17

MY WONDERFUL YEARS
WITH ROYAL DOULTON
CHARACTER JUGS AND FIGURINES

As I often did when my antique pickings got slim, I had inserted a small wanted-to-buy ad in the classified pages of the Chicago *Tribune* and had let it work for me. This time my ad said I was after Mettlach steins, and that I was paying good prices.

Not long after, I received a call from a doctor's wife in Elgin who said she had a fine Mettlach stein to sell. When we arrived at the seller's home, we were asked in. I spotted at once the one-half liter etched Playing Card stein sitting on a table. I walked over to it and asked if I could pick it up.

If I was going to pay $200 for this stein, it had to be perfect. Even a hairline crack could mean a 75% loss. I found the stein to be mint in this case, and paid for it.

As Fran and I were ready to leave, our hostess

pointed to a plate rail all the way around her large kitchen and asked me if I dealt in tobies. I confessed that I hadn't even seen a Royal Doulton toby before seeing hers along the plate rail that day, let alone be a dealer in them.

Royal Doulton character jugs or tobies are handled mugs made in the form of a head, or sometimes a seated figure. Most of them are characters from English history and literature, or street characters.

There were about 50 large tobies up on the rail that our hostess said her husband had paid $8 each for while they were collecting through the 60s. Jokingly, I asked what her price was for the lot. She said she would sell them for $8.50 each.

I talked a bit with Fran about the high price being asked for what I believed was junk. It was because Fran convinced me to buy them that I entered the fascinating Royal Doulton field that would within two or three years lift me to the top of the heap in this country in Royal Doulton.

When I got home with the doctor's wife's tobies, I immediately advertised them with pictures in the *Antique Trader*. It was a correct move. I was deluged with calls asking me if I still had the large Two-Faced Devil shown in my ad. I soon learned it was a $400 toby. The Red-Haired Clown in my ad was a $1,000 toby.

There was only one problem. A dealer friend of mine from Sheridan, Illinois, had come to visit me the day after I brought the tobies home, just before my ad came out. When he offered me $25 each for the 50-toby collection, I sold them to him fast. I cleared almost $1,000 on this quick turn-over, and learned a valuable lesson, that Royal Doulton tobies were in big demand.

One of the callers who answered my ad too late asked me who had purchased the tobies, and like a fool, I gave him the Sheridan dealer's phone number. When I called the dealer a few days later, he told me that my phone caller had driven over from Iowa non-stop and creamed the best of his collection for $75 each, including the Red-Haired Clown and Two-Faced Devil. When I informed him that they were all worth from double that up to **20 times more**, he learned something, too.

In the years that followed, I bought almost all the sizes and kinds of Royal Doulton tobies ever made, and more than any other dealer in the country. I accomplished this by advertising to buy tobies in all of the nation's important antique magazines and papers at once, week after week and year after year.

Advertising is like playing the slots in Las Vegas. If you feed the slots long enough, you're bound to hit the jackpot. So it goes with advertising for the illusive rarities in Royal Doulton tobies, was my belief. I fed the advertising kitty daily until, periodically, I hit the Royal Doulton toby jackpot, and believe you me, I hit some Jim Dandys in my day.

At that time there were about 600 different size tobies. They ranged in size from 1¼″ "teenies" to 5¼″ jugs, and in subjects from Dickens characters to London street persons. Many times I would have so many of these character jugs on hand to sell that they looked like soldiers marching rank on rank to battle on my shelves.

The clear buying field I had at that time made me realize that I had started advertising to buy something that very few dealers in the country knew the prices of. There wasn't a single price guide or listing at that time, nor up to 1977, to turn to for help.

A collector friend whom I had helped get started in Royal Doulton collecting aided me by sending me information on recent toby prices in England, as he travelled back and forth. This made it possible for me to keep my ever-changing weekly buying prices up to date. These weekly buy lists I put out were read by several million readers of all the five major trade magazines and papers in the U.S., and served to whet the appetites of collectors for Royal Doulton character jugs.

They turned to them in droves. Anything that was made so plentifully and for so long as Royal Doulton tobies and figurines was ready to catch on with the American collector, and when it did so, it became one of the nation's No. 1 collectibles.

One day I received a letter from a lady in Panama who wrote that she had a complete collection of the large-size royal Doulton toby jugs for sale. She and her husband had bought them over the years in shops where freighters from England unloaded them. She sold me 100 of the big tobies, or 5¼″ character jugs, including some of the rarest known at that time, for a flat $15 each.

The tobies arrived in four large pasteboard boxes via United Parcel. I got one thrill after another unpacking them when I saw the Devil, Clown, Fortune Teller, Gondolier, Gulliver, 'Ard of 'Earing (very rare, sells for up to $1,200 today even in the miniature size of 2¼″), Hatless Drake, White Churchill, and many of the other rare English friends I had learned to know and love. This kind of a sweet deal was to see itself repeated many times over the next five years.

I saw the White Churchill toby go in price from $100 in 1968 to $10,000 in 1983. I saw the Hatless Drake toby go from $750 in 1973 to $7,500 in 1983. I saw the large Two-Faced Devil go from $500 in 1973 to $2,000 in 1984. As for the Royal Doulton figurines that I began dealing in later, they went up many times in value in just two or three years.

The figurines were introduced to collectors about 1890 with No. l, and today they number about 2,900. Most have their name and H N (house number) on the bottom. The early figurines were made of bone china, giving them a richer and more distinctive look than the later ones.

When I decided to compliment my toby dealings with Royal Doulton figurines, I studied figurine information for six months, and then broke loose in all five of our biggest trade magazines with the biggest advertising blitz that was ever put on by anyone in the history of Royal Doulton trading. I inserted large buy ads that read, "I pay $75 for all old Royal Doulton figurines." I had to put it this way, or it would have taken a mile of advertising space to list the ones I needed.

In reality, those I needed were the discontinued, or out of factory production numbers. The smaller the HN number of the figurine a caller or writer would say he had, the rarer the figurine, the higher the price I would get from my list of buyers. Soon the figurines started to roll in by the hundreds each year.

In 1975, a lady from St. Louis wrote me that she had 600 figurines to sell. I got on the phone immediately, and was told that she would send me a list shortly of the first hundred she would part with. Offhand, she did not remember their names. When the figurine

Two Royal Doulton figurines, Toinette, $1,450; and Leda and the Swan, $2,500.

The Two-Faced Devil toby, large size, $1,600-$2,200.

list came, it nearly made me fall over backwards. Included were many early, discontinued men figurines, which are the most coveted of all because of their scarcity. My seller listed HN 2084, King Charles; HN 356, Sir Thomas Lovell; HN 2134, An Old King; HN 317, Shylock; HN 688, A Yeoman of the Guard, and many more.

Also included were what dealers call the Eight Queens, depicted wearing their beautiful ball gowns and other finery of the period. They are HN 2005, Henrietta Maria; HN 2006, The Lady Anne Nevill; HN 2007, Mrs. Fitzherbert; HN 2008, Philippa of Hainault; HN 2009, Eleanor of Provence; HN 2110, the Young Miss Nightingale; HN 2011, Matilda; and HN 2012, Margaret of Anjou.

The reason for the high price of the queens is that they were only in production for five years after World War II, 1948-53. The set will get a lot higher before it ever goes lower. I have bought and sold single queens out of the set several times, but only once, in the days when Royal Doulton was my specialty, did I manage to buy a complete set.

I sold the set soon after its purchase from the St. Louis seller. It went to a New Jersey dealer for $2,000. I made $400 on the deal. If I had kept this set, today I could sell it for several times more.

To date almost 2,900 different men and lady figurines have been put out by the Royal Doulton factory at Burselm, England. At one time or another in my ten years as a Doulton specialist, I owned almost all the figurines made above HN 2,000, a good record that I am proud of. Royal Doulton figurine collecting is simplified by the fact that each one has its name and HN affixed under the glaze on the base. A collector has simply to see the name and HN in an ad to know that he will receive exactly what is ordered and not a white elephant.

I soon made enough profit on figurines to buy an expensive car. For the first time in my life there were no bill collectors knocking at my door. With six hungry mouths at the table, belonging to my two beautiful girls and two good-looking boys, as well as to Fran and myself, it was gratifying to be able to buy anything they needed. Fran was allowed to buy an expensive pair of shoes and a moderately priced dress. I was acquiring a taste for better food at restaurants. After I was introduced to baked oyster Rockefeller by friends, I would order it every Friday at the beautiful Nachusa House Hotel in Dixon.

In 1976, Katherine Morrison McClinton, author of around 20 books on antiques, wrote and asked me if I would help her with her new book, *Royal Doulton Figurines and Character Jugs*. I helped her for over a year with photos of great Doulton rarities and inside information about both the charming figurines and the handsome tobies. Many of the photos in the book are of tobies in my collection, and I am listed among five top dealers and collectors in the country who helped with the book.

One day in 1970 when my Royal Doulton ads were running in about 16 national trade papers, I received a letter from a lady telling me she had for sale one of the White-Haired Clowns I was seeking and paying $175 for. I wrote and told her to send it, saying I would mail her a cashier's check the moment it arrived.

When the Clown arrived a few days later and I opened the box, I couldn't believe what I saw, a cheap reproduction (I thought), and not even of a white-haired clown, but of a phony-looking Red-Haired Clown. I debated whether to send it right back and not pay, telling the sender it was a repro. However, I decided to try it out first on a buyer.

I immediately called a customer in Missouri to tell him I had just gotten in a 3¼″ Two-Faced Devil toby, priced at $175, and also had just bought a White-Haired Clown that he might be interested in, priced at $250. My customer, who at that time possessed an almost complete collection of tobies, said yes to both.

Three or four days later Fran answered the phone and told me my Missouri customer wanted to talk to me. My hands trembled as I walked to the phone, expecting that he would chew me out for screwing up his order. I held the receiver a little distance from my ear to soften the loud lambasting I was sure I'd receive.

I told my customer, "I'm sorry I sent you a red-haired toby instead of the white one."

"Don't be sorry, Dan," he said, "you have topped off my 20-year search for the toby I needed to complete my collection. I will always be grateful to you for sending me the Red-Haired Clown. If there is anything I can ever do for you, please do not hesitate to call me day or night."

I then hung up the receiver, and with my mouth still hanging open, I began to ask myself, what had I done to make this very advanced toby collector so happy?

A few months later I was advertising to buy the Red-Haired Clown for $1,000, which explains why my customer was so happy. He got a real bargain. The Red-Haired Clown is just plain ugly, but this ugliness soon fades when you look at your Red-Haired Clown and know you can cash it in for $5,000 today.

I had sold a lot of antiques and collectibles up to that time, but never did I sell anything as short as I did that ugly Red-Haired Clown, the only toby that looked so bad to the Royal Doulton factory that production on it was halted almost before it got started, causing it to be a great rarity and high-priced today.

I was going along at a fast clip in 1976, when that fall, I saw the beginning of the end. I went out of the Royal Doulton and Mettlach stein mail-order business both at once and for the same reason, vast over-pricing by other dealers.

First one, and then two and more Ohio Doulton dealers went into a trade journal with their big buy ads similar to mine, but offering $50 to $250 more for each character jug or figurine than my ads stated I'd pay. This immediately made me raise my buy price, and I had to do it over and over for the balance of 1976. (I never once needed to run an ad to sell a toby or figurine, having a list of wealthy customers who would buy all I could locate.)

I tried to influence the Ohio dealers through friends of mine to stop cutting each other's throats with this weekly price raise, but to no avail. I couldn't help but wonder what these hungry young dealers were doing with the tobies and figurines they were buying, since they never advertised any for sale. I learned they were selling to clients that were investing in all the Doulton tobies and figurines they could find.

Not being able to pay the higher and higher weekly prices that were being advertised, I folded up my Royal Doulton tent and rode off into the lonesome desert after almost a decade of holding down the Nation's No. 1 spot as a Royal Doulton dealer.

18

HOW THE MIAMI MAFIA
GOT INTO MY
TIFFANY ACT

In 1975, fine Tiffany lamps had just begun their ascendancy to the ultimate in lamps, and I wanted to get in on the action. It was just about that time I got a call from a dealer and old friend at Elizabeth, Illinois, who told me he knew of a signed Tiffany lamp for sale. It was owned by a man who had just moved to the country near there from Chicago. My friend said he would send me a picture of the lamp.

When I saw the picture, I immediately got the owner on the phone to see if I could drive the 60 miles from Dixon to buy the lamp. I got the go-ahead and the driving instructions. I wasted no time in jumping in my new car that I had bought with profits from my Mettlach dealing, and went out on the prowl for the biggest antique game I had stalked in my life.

The more I thought about how much I was going

to make on the lamp if I was able to buy it from the rough-sounding Chicago-bred owner, the harder my foot pressed on the gas pedal, until once or twice I almost turned over on the crooked blacktop.

I finally wheeled into a large farmyard with the house set back of a big lawn. I didn't need to knock at the door, because Arnold Biggs was watching for me, drinking scotch and looking out his screened porch door. After we had shaken hands and talked awhile, Biggs said he would show me the lamp, and led me to an old trailer at one side of the yard.

"You'll have to look at the lamp the way it is in here," he said. "We haven't had any electricity connected out here since Mother died two years ago. The lamp was hers, she bought it in Chicago back in the 20's. I have always remembered her saying that it was a Tiffany lamp and worth a lot of money."

I couldn't begin to hide the thrill I got as I looked through the trailer door to the far end and saw standing on a table the most magnificent lamp of any type that I had ever seen. A tulip garden seemed to start at the edge of the shade in light pinks, and then gradually turned redder and redder until in a full crescendo of dark red tulips, the shade turned flaming red at its crown. You have to see such a lamp to feel the impact of its dazzling beauty.

I asked Biggs if I could look under the shade for cracks in the 1,000 or more tulip panels. He said, "Sure, go ahead." I was not looking for cracks, but rather for the small half-dime-sized bronze seal saying "Tiffany Studios, N.Y." It was there, attached right inside the lamp rim as it was supposed to be. I then asked Biggs if I could unscrew the wing piece at the crown and take the shade off to see if the base was solid brass. He again told me to go ahead, but be careful. I was careful, all right. As I turned the lamp base up and away from the owner, I saw what I was looking for, the Tiffany Studios signature on the base, with the number to match the top.

With that, I got the show on the road. I suspected that Biggs was not going to be a problem, since he didn't know or care enough to examine his mother's gorgeous lamp to see if it was signed Tiffany or anything else. I asked, "What will you take for your lamp?"

Biggs said he didn't know anything about Tiffany lamps or any other kind. He said if I wanted to buy his lamp, to make him an offer.

I didn't want to bid too little for the gorgeous Tiffany and risk a chance of his getting mad and asking me to leave. Neither did I want to overbid and lose a lot of my profit. Should I bid high or bid low? I chose to bid in between. I told the Chicago man, "I can pay you $4,500 for your mother's lamp. How will that be?"

Biggs looked through me as only an ex-Chicago travelling salesman could in sizing up a customer, and to my disbelief said, "It's yours."

I couldn't begin to contain my relief and joy at being able to buy this rare, mint Tiffany lamp, and I was even more eager to get it quickly out of there and safely home. Biggs accepted my personal check for the $4,500, which I thought was strange. He explained that the Elizabeth dealer had told him I was OK. (I later paid that dealer $750 for his lead.)

The Tiffany lamp was 28″ high, and with its 25″-wide tulip floral 1,000 panel shade, it was not only heavy, but bulky. Where, I though, could I put it in my Eldorado coupe? It was too big for the back seat, so I decided to put it in the trunk. I first removed the spare tire and took the felt cloth wrapper off it, and put that loosely around the lamp shade, and then I carried it to the car trunk and set it carefully down on its rim. Man, I surely didn't want to injure this big cream puff of a shade now, after it had been cared for for almost 75 years by the Biggs and whoever had owned it previously.

But before I could leave, I was invited into the house to see Biggs' collection of primitive pine furniture circa 1800-1840, plus old duck decoys, crocks, and all the rest of his inherited farm treasures. While seeing this collection was interesting, I couldn't stop thinking of getting out of his place fast.

Biggs then brought out a fifth of Chivas Regal scotch and invited me to have a drink. This was just the brand of drink I was on at that time, and I had to tell Biggs what a big coincidence that was. I asked him, then, what he thought of the bid I had made on his lamp.

He said, "Shiaras," as he gulped a big shot of scotch, "if you had bid a nickle less, I'd have kicked you out of the trailer."

I could see as he straightened up to his full 6′ 2″ height, with his seamed, hard face, plain work clothes, and over-sized cowboy boots, that he could do just what he said. This kind of talk made me even more anxious to exit the place. But Biggs insisted I have two or three more jolts of the Chivas Regal. In the meantime I was reflecting that as long as I was parked in his yard, he could pull out a gun and order me to remove the great Tiffany rarity out onto his lawn.

Finally I was able to say good-bye. What a big relief to get off the property! Once I was out on the road,

I felt that the greatest lamp ever to surface in that area and the highest priced, was mine. I drove home much more slowly that I had come. I carried my big-game-hunt quarry, the leaded Tiffany, in the door and placed it on a specially-waiting marble-topped table.

The dealer who had tipped me off told me later that Biggs had received an offer of $15,000 for the lamp one day after I had purchased it. This was in response to a colored photo he had sent to a dealer in the East. Once more I had moved fast enough.

After a day or two of admiring the lamp, I sent photos of it to a long-time Tiffany dealer friend for an exact appraisal. A reply came in a few days with an appraisal of $13,500. At that time, any five-digit figure was considered high. Today this lamp would sell for about $30,000 to $40,000.

The lamp was called the Red Tulip, my friend told me, and gave me the catalogue number. I cannot describe how beautiful my Red Tulip Tiffany table lamp was to me. The leaded favrile glass that Tiffany had invented in the 1890's at his New York studio was used in the lamp. This invention had its own inner beauty, that seemed to make any shape formed by it look alive and ready to leap out at the viewer. The 1,000 different-shaded glass panels seemed to form a sea of flaming red tulips put together so beautifully with bronze welding that I swore I was in a real red tulip garden every time I lit it.

Once I had the appraisal made, I was ready to advertise the lamp in a national paper. I deliberately made up one of my largest photo ads with about 16 photos, and in the lower corner I inserted a tiny photo of what I believed was the greatest signed lamp ever to be advertised in that trade paper up to that time.

I then sat back and waited for a customer to bite. I didn't have long to wait when a call came from the greater Miami area. After I described the lamp, the caller said quickly that he would buy it. He told me he was a dealer in Tiffany lamps, and had about 100 Tiffany, Handel, and Pairpoint lamps on hand.

After we had talked over the price, my buyer said he would fly to O'Hare Field in Chicago, and suggested we meet at a motel room. I asked instead that he meet me with the money at my cousin's home in Norridge, a town just one mile from O'Hare. My cousin was a cop in that city, and he had agreed to let me use his house for the big lamp transaction.

When I got there with Fran, we parked the car in the drive and brought all the tulips inside to safety. I don't trust Chicago with a necktie in my car.

Soon a knock came at the door, and it was my buyer from Miami. He said a friend was coming down from Detroit to look at the lamp with him and would be there in a few minutes. Just like clockwork, in another ten minutes the second man was at the door. He was introduced as a Tiffany specialist who had been hired by my buyer to make certain all the over-1,000 panels were original Tiffany favrile and that nothing had been replaced or repaired.

While the expert stooped over the lamp examining the panels one by one, I said to myself, I thought my buyer was an experienced Tiffany lamp man himself, and he should know all this about replaced or repaired glass panels. All of a sudden I grew apprehensive that I was going to get the "bad lamp" treatment, with the intent of telling me it was a repaired lamp, and then convincing me to take maybe $7,500 or $10,000 for it instead of full price. I kept looking at my cousin, the cop, who had worked the rackets for many years; but his look said all was OK with this pair. I guess he could tell, after taking hundreds of the slippery types into headquarters and interrogating them in depth in the squad room.

I felt considerably better after the men stood up following their hour of closely inspecting the lamp and called it OK. With this, my Miami dealer pulled out the sum of money we had agreed on over the phone and paid me. I told him to use the big boxes that we had piled in the driveway for packing, but he said they would carry the lamp on the plane as it was and asked my cousin for a ride to the airport.

On the way to O'Hare, one man held the big shade on his lap, while the other held the heavy bronze base between his legs. When my cousin tried to get something out of them about the lamp's destination, they revealed that it was going to a Mafia mobster's wife. The Mafia was investing a lot of money in Tiffany lamps, they told him. My cousin figured both of the guys were working for the Syndicate, and had orders from their Mafia chief to bring back the lamp to his home if it was mint.

The Mafia, I believe, had obtained secret information as to the possibility of making big money on Tiffany, and was advised to buy, buy, buy.

The two men boarded the plane carrying the lamp shade and base. They must have paid out some good money for personnel to look the other way.

It wasn't long after I sold this lamp that the Tiffany table lamp market blew its top off, with a great Spiderweb Tiffany breaking a record when it sold for $250,000 at Sotheby's in New York. About the same time a beautiful Dragonfly Tiffany sold for $200,000 and a Laburnum went for $85,000 at Sotheby's.

I can still see the sea of red tulips in the lamp I sold, put together so artistically by the Tiffany artists. It is a great lamp that I know the Mafia Chieftain's wife, if she still owns it today, must thank me for selling.

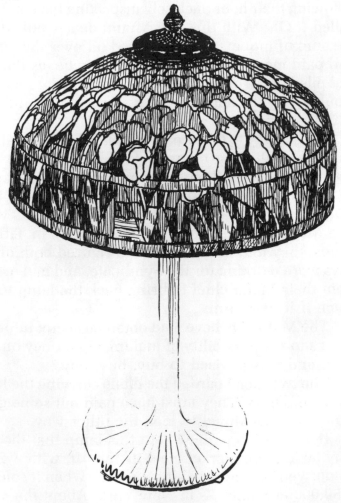

The Red Tulip Tiffany, $30,000-$40,000.

19

WHEN A RARE TOY
BECOMES
JUST A TOY

Back in the mid-1960's, old cast iron and tin toys really took off price-wise, and they haven't been headed yet. Boys will always be boys, and come hell or high water, they must have antique toys to look at, if not to play with, at prices that would stagger your imagination.

I used to look harder for good toys at sales than for any other antique, and I found a lot of them. The first big toy collection I was offered belonged to a Rock Falls, Illinois, dealer. As I was escorted into her antique toy room, I could hardly grasp at first the amount of high quality toys displayed. There were scores of near-mint German Lehman wind-up tin toys, plus Lionel and American Flyer electric trains, and a two-foot-long cast iron fire pumper with horses. She said they had all come from the city dump.

"You mean you went out to the dump and found all these toys?" I asked the elderly lady.

"They all came from the guard there who sees that the garbage is dumped in the right place," she said. She told me that every time a likely-looking truck would begin to dump boxes that might have toys, the guard would go through them. He had worked almost 50 years as a watchman, looking through a zillion loads of often stinking garbage, to find the more than 200 toys on the shelves.

Thinking I would try to swipe them from the dealer at a low price, I asked what she wanted for the Ives cast iron horses and pumper wagon. There wasn't any hesitation--$375! I couldn't understand where she had found such up-to-date prices for every last thing. She quoted me $75 for all the signed German Lehman toys, and I couldn't get this much for them in the East.

I am currently selling the better Lehman toys for $375 to $600 when I can find them. It was not a bit unusual in the mid-60's to find a Lehman tin wind-up marked Germany for $15 at a farm sale. I would send all I could find to a Kansas City dealer who, after 20 years, is still seeking all the Lehmans he can buy through ads in the trade papers.

The best electric train to invest your money in today is the 1920's Lionel. The Lionel standard gauge train has a 3"-wide track and many times is over eight feet in length. It usually has 10"-long observation, passenger, and baggage cars, with a red caboose behind. The condition of the paint and overall appearance have a big bearing on what to pay. In the old days I could often buy one of these Lionels for $50. Now the price is often $1000.

There is something about an electric train that

makes men go nuts to own it. I have bought a lot of
Lionel standard gauge trains and hundreds of the HO
trains, and on not one did I fail to make a good profit.
I advertised the standard Lionel train #518 in completely rusted out condition around six months ago,
thinking I was not going to get a nibble at $400. The
rare set sold immediately to a train restorer in Buf-
falo, New York. Here is a case of a person so devoted
to his train hobby that he would take perhaps a year
to restore a rusty train to like-new condition.

In the mechanical and "still" bank field is where
I mixed with Al Sidwell, who for 30 years had been
writing monthly articles about banks in a trade
magazine out of Chicago. For many years "Sid" would
call me up once or twice a week around 11 p.m., and
we would swap toy and banks news. Sid bought many
mint banks and toys from me over the five or six years
when I could still find them. Today he owns the biggest collection in the U.S. of everything good in the
bank and toy field.

I also did a lot of selling to the late Art Tiller from
Cincinnati, Ohio, who once owned the biggest collection of still banks in the U.S. The last time I saw him
was at a bank sale north of Cincinnati, where the
banks and toys had been grossly exaggerated as to
grading. The best banks were only repaints, and the
mechanical penny banks had in many instances been
touched up where they were professionally repaired.
You couldn't fool Tiller on repaints and repairs. He
said, "Dan, I wouldn't take a repaired or repainted cast
iron penny bank if it was given me free."

This is a good point to remember. You should not
buy a repaired or repainted toy of any kind, let alone
1880's toy banks.

There were some rare banks bringing big prices even 15 years ago. At that time, the rarest bank in the world, the Old Lady in the Shoe bank, used to sell for $10,000. Recently one was purchased for $50,000. Many other mechanical banks carry price tags right next door to this.

There are around 3,000 known cast iron still banks dating from 1885 to 1910. Back in 1971 I bought over 100 cast iron still banks from a retired state cop, paying $1,375, and crying all the while I was buying them that I couldn't make a dime on them. I thought I would advertise them as a lot in a trade paper to see if there was any serious cast iron still bank money in the country. To my surprise I received at least a dozen calls to buy them, and finally sold them to a big New York contractor for a good profit. He wrote me later how pleased he was that they were all the genuine article and not the phonies some other dealers in the trade had sent him and which he quickly returned.

If you are not familiar with what the real McCoy looks like in an old bank, you had better not buy. Some close friends of mine who have started collecting still banks in the past two or three years, have bought nothing but junk repros. Instead of buying from a reputable dealer, they have patronized fly-by-night flea market dealers, who are many times from out of state and don't hesitate to stick someone with a $50 or higher reproduction.

There is no sure way to avoid the pitfall of buying reproduction banks other than to deal with established dealers. The fly-by-nights take a new bank and bury it in the ground for about three weeks until the metal has just started to get rusted and has that old look they desire. Then on their flea market shelf it goes, waiting for a sucker to come along. Many times I have seen a poor novice collector taken to the cleaners for as much as $400 or $500 for new mechanical banks that are being produced even more widely than the stills.

If you want to be a cast iron bank or toy collector, first go to a reputable dealer and buy a genuine bank or toy to look at several times a week. Pick it up and examine the paint and the way it was molded. This will help you in recognizing a repro.

I check a bank to see if it is old by looking carefully at the way it has been molded, especially on the bottom of the feet of the person or animal it represents, and comparing it mentally with a bank I know to be old. I check the base to see if it shows even, smooth wear, and the paint job to see if it is aged in appearance. Mostly, I rely on the person I buy from. I can almost always tell if a bank is authentic, but I will admit I am afraid of toy banks, even though I have been dealing in them for 30 years.

The mechanical banks, of which there are over 300, are for my bucks more fun to collect than money in the bank. Most of them will sell for over $600. Nearly all are reproduced.

The mechanicals do many things as you place a penny in their slot. A baseball player will pitch the penny at the catcher in the Darktown Battery mechanical bank, which I have bought and sold several times. Another bank is called the Eagle and Eaglets. When you put a penny in the mother eagle's mouth, she will put her head down and feed the eaglets at her feet. The William Tell bank shoots a penny into an apple on a boy's head at the far end of the range. The dentist bank simulates the pulling of a tooth, and on it goes.

As for other toys, the German tin toys circa 1890-1930 are the most desirable. A few years ago a 31"-long tin steamboat made by the Bing Co. of Germany sold for $31,000 at a New York city auction gallery.

You can learn a lot about what is going on in toys by subscribing to *Toy World* magazine out of Chicago. You will see how all the toy greats of the country buy their fine cast iron and German-made toys. The one toy that will surprise you if you should come across it is the Lionel Donald Duck handcar, which sells for over $800 at auction. The Lionel Mickey and Minnie handcar is a shoo-in to sell for $600. The Amos 'n' Andy 1930's Fresh-Air Taxi tin wind-up sells in the East for $600.

In the summer of 1981 I was sitting in my office working on a new ad when the phone rang and the caller told me he had 8,500 fine old toys to sell. I thought the man must be daft, but I thought I would listen to his story. He said he was calling from nearby Sterling, and would call back the next morning with directions, if I would like to buy all or part of them.

The next morning my caller suggested I meet him at 2 p.m. that afternoon in a fast-food parking lot. I agreed, but began to worry it might be a set-up like a Rockford dealer had walked into the year before. He went to an apartment where he had an appointment and was zapped over the head, all his money taken, and was left to bleed to death on the floor of the shoddy flat that had been rented just to rob him. I worried that I might get the same treatment if I went alone, so I called my sometimes-partner, Nate Ross, who took the afternoon off from his sales job just to see what might be going on over in Sterling. He came packing a revolver in his hip pocket, and for this I was thankful.

We drove to the designated parking lot but it was empty except for one car with occupants having sandwiches. We looked all around, and then we saw a man waving to us from the third floor of an adjacent building. We walked over to the iron steps that went almost straight up, and I let Nate go up first. After climbing almost 25 feet of steps, he walked into the building and then after a moment he came back out and waved his hand for me to come on up.

When I got to the top of the iron steps, I could see, through the open door of the warehouse, five rows of toys that stretched for the entire 250 feet of the room. When I got inside, I saw that rows of toys five shelves deep extended the length of the other side of the room as well. Covering the warehouse floor were large Buddy L and Structo steel toys, and at least 200 large and small electric train sets.

One section of the shelf space was full of still and mechanical banks. The next section had hundreds of bisque dolls, and at the rear of the building were children's cast iron cook stoves in every shape and size you could think of. There was one big section after another full of 1900 German tin wind-up toys, and then came the 1920's and 1930's American-made tin wind-ups like the Amos 'n' Andy Fresh-Air Taxi, Highway Henry, and Ferdinand the Bull wind-ups.

By this time I recognized the collections and knew the owners. They had not divulged their names because we had had some unsatisfactory dealings in the past, and they knew I would not have come to see their toys had I known who was calling. I asked Nate if we should try to buy something just to see what they were charging.

I picked up an Andy Gump bank and a couple of

Lehman toys to get some sample prices. I had to give the number on each toy, and then by using a file, the owners quickly came up with prices of $800 and $725. I bought them and Nate and I hurriedly left the premises.

When I got home I found the bank had some damage that would cost me $400, and the 1900 Lehman tin wind-up toys were listed at less than any other toy Lehman made.

Later, I heard, the partners got into it and sold the toys at auction in the East, losing their shirts. I, too, lost around $300.

This story is told to advise you not to go on calls that are vague and mysterious. Every day one reads of someone getting mugged for a wallet, let alone for the amount of cash that it is required for a dealer to carry when dealing away from home. Make the seller bring his antiques to your place of business, or tell him to meet you half-way at your car. You could be making your last antique call when you go into a strange home with cash in your pocket.

Good luck in hunting fine old toys. It is a fun hobby that never ceases to make one happy.

A rare toy becomes just a toy:

. . . when you let Nephew Up and At 'Em play with it, damaging the paint. A mint Amos 'n' Andy Fresh-Air Taxi toy circa 1936 is worth $600 mint. In the original packing carton, $1,200. With only 80% paint, $300 to $400. A mint 18″ Shirley Temple doll sells for $400. In her original blue ribbon shipping carton, she will bring $650. If damaged, 30 to 40% less.

. . . when you let Niece Rough and Ready

crack or chip it. A fine German character Simon Halbig doll with star mark on the back of her bisque head may sell for $600 to $800, but if her face or head is cracked, the value drops to only a few hundred. To bring top-dollars, dolls must be mint, and this includes the body as well as the dainty bisque hands. One finger chip and your doll is going to be discounted or even rejected at a doll auction. Collectors will pay double and triple for almost any antique if absolutely mint.

. . . when it has been repaired. No one will give much for a repaired toy that you want to dispose of.

. . . when it shows rusted areas. A toy with only a small amount of rust or pitting may be sent back to you in the mail-order business.

Therefore, if possible, buy only the cream, and leave the whey for the next guy in this wonderful world of toy collecting.

One of the rarest of banks, *Old Woman In The Shoe, $50,000.* When coin is placed in slot and lever pulled, old lady punishes children. *(From photo furnished by Stephen Stectbeck, Ft. Wayne, Indiana.)*

Rocking Horse, $400-$450.

20

THE ST. PAUL, MINNESOTA, METTLACH STEIN HEIST

There are over 1,200 different Mettlach steins, and at one time or another, I have owned most of them. During the years that I was the best-known Mettlach dealer in the nation, I was on the move constantly throughout the U.S. buying up big and small Mettlach collections that my ads brought to light. During those years, 1963 to 1977, when I would go to auctions, the auctioneer would say, "Here comes Mr. Mettlach."

The Mettlach factory had its beginnings in 1767 when a pottery was founded near Luxemberg, Germany, by Pierre Joseph Boch. Later Pierre's son started a pottery at Mettlach. The two factories and one operated by Nicholas Villeroy consolidated in 1841. This organization developed the decorated stonewares that became known the world over as Mettlach.

The Benedictine Abbey of Mettlach was purchased

and used as a factory. Included in the purchase was the famous Old Tower which, from around 1882, served as a trademark for nearly every piece made there. To this day, the abbey's central building continues to serve as the main production facility.

By 1838, 75 workers were employed at the factory. An art school for the staff was opened in 1851. During the period 1882 to 1910, a tremendous variety of colors, each with its own formula code number, was used. There were 150 under-glaze colors, 30 colored clay slips, and 176 different colored glazes.

The highest priced Mettlach steins are the chromolith (variously called etched, incised, or engraved) stoneware. Because of loss of records due to a factory fire in 1921, the exact process for the chromolith Mettlach beer steins is not known today. In these steins, the variously colored clays are kept separate to form very intricate designs. In most cases, the different colored sections are separated by engraved lines colored black, which gives the individual areas distinctive emphasis and detail.

As an indication of how high a place Mettlach occupies in the stein world, the most important guest at our annual convention of the Stein Club International, held in 1982 at St. Charles, Illinois, was Dr. Teresa Thomas, director of the Mettlach Archives and Museum. The stein club membership is made up of 1,161 stein collectors from all over the world.

Steins were originally made to drink beer out of, and they had a lid to keep the flies out. Without a lid, it is not a stein. Mettlach steins range in size from ¼ liter to seven liters. The big ones, of around four liters or over, are krugs or trophy steins. They were given in varying sizes to Mettlach workers as they retired.

Here are some current prices for a few of the steins that I have sold from 1963 to 1975.

1. Mettlach No. 2764, 6 liter, 24″ tall. Knight sitting on a white horse and drinking from a stein. Coloring of vivid blues, white, and burnt umber. Signed Heinrich Schlitt. Known as the *White Horse*. $6,400. I have owned this rare stein three times.

2. No. 2478, 5 liter, 24″ tall. Body of stein is knights in armor on horses, with castle in the background. Lid is turret of tan stone. This is the *Hildebrand* stein. $5,750. I owned this great cameo stein one time.

3. No. 2455, 6.8 liter, 26″ tall. Pewter knight in armor holding shield on lid. Swans around base. Holy Grail above scene radiating light. The *Lohengren* stein. $4,600. I sold this stein once for $2,000 in the 1972-75 years.

4. No. 2038, 3.8 liter, 16″ tall. Body is composed of green treetops with housetops showing above them. Mettlach Abbey with well in courtyard forms the lid. The *Black Forest* stein. $6,000. I have owned this great krug one time.

Once during our stein-buying years, my wife and I drove 400 miles non-stop to get in the door first and beat the competition to a seller's home.

We had received a letter from a St. Paul, Minnesota, lady in reply to my steins-wanted ad. She wrote that she had for sale 110 Mettlach steins and much more. I got on the phone immediately and when I learned she had written another dealer as well about the collection, I asked her not to answer any phone calls until I got there. I gave my wife just a few minutes notice to be ready to leave.

I knew from the order numbers of the steins listed in the letter, and the prices asked, that the letter was either a big mistake or a joke. A rival stein dealer in St. Paul would pull just such a prank on me to make me go on a wild goose chase of 800 miles round trip.

As we made the drive, I reflected on the fact that the St. Paul lady had also written an Atlanta, Georgia, dealer, who had advertised for steins as well. Thinking of the ridiculously low prices at which the steins were being offered, I imagined the rival dealer already in her house creaming her collection.

The time was April, but as we pulled into St. Paul with our station wagon carrying a load of cardboard packing boxes in the back, there was still snow on the ground. I got out of the car before a modest home and told Fran, "If I don't wave out the door to you that this is on the level, go bring the police, for I might be in very serious trouble."

As the door opened, I nearly keeled over at what I saw. Standing in rows in glass show-cases were many of the rare one-half and one-liter steins that the Mettlach factory had made from 1885 to 1905, their best production years. I went right to work, waving my hand at Fran to park the wagon and come in. The next two or so hours were going to be the most profitable, as well as the most fun, of my Mettlach career.

All of the rarer half-liter and one-liter David and Goliath, Black Forest, and White Horse steins were wrapped up and packed first, at such a low price that I was choking and clearing my throat constantly at this wholesale robbery. I quickly figured that both versions of the rare one liter Black Forest, which the owner was asking $400 for, could be sold immediately to a Chicago doctor for $1,200 each. So a profit of $1,600 was assured for these two. In addition, the doctor would probably buy the two rare one-half liter

Black Forests, priced at $450 each, for $750 each. A grand total of $2,200 profit was already in the bag in one of the biggest and best buys ever heard of among Mettlach dealers up to this time. In fact, as far as I know, nothing like this stein sale has ever occurred again, and it will remain in my memory as the Great Mettlach Stein Heist.

Next, I walked swiftly over to No. 2038, the rare 3.8 liter Black Forest krug stein which the seller wrote me she had bought for her son (just then standing in the back of the room) as a birthday present some years before. She had paid $550, and true to her letter, she had marked it $650, giving herself a $100 profit. What she did not know was that she had insured me a $3,000 profit with that price; because that stein, at the time, was coveted as much as any of the Mettlach steins, surpassing even the great White Horse No. 2765 six-liter 24″-tall krug, which today is twice as valuable, if not three times.

Before the afternoon had ended I had bought all 110 of the etched Mettlach steins, and Fran kept packing them in cardboard boxes as we went. I could have made a lot more money that day but I could not pay in cash, and the seller finally called a halt to how many steins she would sell me by check. This was a shame, because the sweet lady and her son had some very rare regimental steins for sale, as well as rarest-of-the-rare two and three-liter German-made colored glass steins with cranberry and emerald green enameling, made before the turn of the century.

While we were buying out the stein collection, the phone must have rung at least 15 or 20 times, but true to her word, the gracious lady seller did not answer, and the Atlanta dealer was whipped.

We loaded up our steins with only my personal check as payment. My reputation as a well-known Mettlach dealer had preceded me, or it would not have been possible.

I took one last look at all the colored glass steins standing so beautifully in a wall-length show-case, along with the dozen or more rare German World War I-era regimentals that included naval, air, and submarine versions. They were among the most valuable I had ever seen. I had to be satisfied with buying the rare William Tells, David and Goliath, and White Horse steins, priced at an average of $100 and worth in some cases $800 to $1,200. You will have to remember, that if I hadn't been buying them, it would have been the Atlanta dealer.

Before we left, I asked the St. Paul lady how she had arrived at her prices. She told me that for years, when she and her son would go to large antique shows to buy steins, they would note the selling prices of all steins like those they owned. Then each year they would average the prices asked by various dealers for each stein. It happened that their average date that April in 1972 came just before Bob Mohr's new price guide on Mettlach steins came out, showing a hefty increase of double and triple what they had been worth the previous year.

We got out of town as fast as our car would take us. I had written a check on an account that needed a hell of a lot of added cash to cover the big check I had handed the sellers. If it had been me doing the selling, I would have called the buyer's bank before any steins were packed to see if there was enough funds to clear the check.

Early next morning I was down at my bank to

transfer money from savings to checking. As I stood at the teller's cage, I happened to glance to my left, and there at the adjacent teller's window was my stein-seller from St. Paul. He must have driven all night to get to Dixon and be at my bank the minute it opened. It was lucky for him I was there, or he wouldn't have been paid one cent.

After the St. Paul man stuffed the big wad of cash in his pocket, we shook hands. He told me he and his mother were not going to sell any more steins. They both had missed the ones they had sold me the moment we drove away.

I learned later that in another two days the rest of the steins were all sold to my St. Paul competitor. The dealer from Georgia had phoned him and told him to go see the steins. Finding the bulk of them gone, he had made short work of all the rest.

The Black Forest, 3.8 liters, $4,500-$5,500.

21

THE MICKEY MANTLE
#311 BASEBALL GUM CARD
TRUE STORY

One day in 1980, I bought a barrel half full of old baseball cards from a lady in Dakota, Illinois, who said her son didn't want them anymore. I hadn't seen a baseball card sell up until that time, so whatever I offered her for them, I thought, was way too much. I paid her $50.

When I got the cards home, I counted over 10,000 cards in fine condition. I advertised them and sold the lot almost immediately on the West Coast. I figured to myself, if there is such a good demand for cards, I will run some local papers, and then placed an ad in the Chicago *Tribune*. My ad read, "I love Mickey Mantle, and will buy all the #311 Mickey Mantle baseball bubble gum cards I can get for $2,000 apiece."

By this time I had learned a little about baseball trading cards. Trading cards were first made by cigarette companies in the 1880's and featured many subjects. Baseball later came to be the favorite, and hundreds of different companies got into the act in the 1930's to 1950's, including gum, bread, beer, and cookie companies, packaging the cards with their product. Certain cards were destined to be more valuable than others because fewer were printed. The cards ranged from domino-size to five by eight inches and larger. Letter designations according to type of company issuing them were given by a pioneer hobbyist, Jefferson Burdick, beginning in 1939. For example, T stands for 20th century tobacco cards, and R for recent gum and candy cards.

Among the most popular cards were those issued by Topps gum in 1952 and 1953. There are 407 baseball subjects in a 1952 Topps Gum baseball card set. Numbers 1 to 310 are worth on an average only about $2 or $3 apiece if mint, while numbers 311 to 407, of which fewer were made, are much more valuable, with a mint Mickey Mantle #311, worth as much as $3,500, being the rarest card in the set. Numbers 312, 313, 350, 400, and 407 are all worth from $150 to $750, with the complete set retailing in 1980 for $10,000. Not bad if you happen to have saved your Topps Bubble Gum cards in 1952. So, you can see how big this nationwide business of collecting old baseball gum cards really is.

It wasn't long after my *Tribune* ad appeared that I received a call from a Chicago-area lady asking me if it was the Mickey Mantle with a bat over his shoulder that I was looking for. I answered yes, and she then told me that she had the card. A date for inspection was set--at 1 p.m. the next day.

When I got out of the car at the specified address, I

told Fran, "If I don't come out of the house in three minutes and give you a wig-wag signal that everything is all right, take off and get the cops."

I was not the only one that was apprehensive.

As I walked up the sidewalk, a big navy officer stepped out wearing a side-arm. I was kept at bay outside the door for five or ten minutes while he questioned me about why I would pay so much for a single baseball card.

After we got to know each other a little better, he told me he had thought I was probably a lunatic to offer $2,000 for a single baseball card, and this was why he put on his revolver. He had seen my ad in the classified section of the **Tribune** while drinking beer the Sunday before, and had remembered he had a cigar box full of vintage cards in his garage. His wife had threatened many times to give them away, but he had insisted each time that he still wanted them. He had also resisted requests from his son, who had wanted to pass the cards out to friends in the neighborhood. The answer had always been no, because he had a sentimental attachment to them. Earlier he had even driven his family to Virginia to his boyhood home to rescue his cards, which his mother had threatened to throw away.

I was finally invited into the house and met the captain's cute young wife, while Fran sat in the car. As we waited for the captian to get Mickey, his wife told me how many times she had been tempted to give the cards away to the kids in the block.

When the officer put Mantle #311 on the table, I could see at a glance that the card was absolutely mint. "Mint" in a baseball card means all the corners are razor-sharp and there are no creases, stains, or abrasions. This, I knew, meant it was worth $1,000 more than the $2,500 which excellent-grade cards were selling for.

After a little small talk, I bought the Mantle, and when the officer finished stuffing the $2,000 in his pocket, I asked if he had any more cards for sale. He said he had some in his bedroom. He went out again, and brought in a cigar box full of 1952 and 1953 Topp cards for me to examine. I riffled through them swiftly to see if any of the 1952 Topps high numbers were there. Not only where they all there, but all the numbers below Mantle #311 were there, too.

I then did the same with the 1953 mint Topps set to see if the star cards were there, and sure enough, there was the Willie Mays #244 card selling for $600 and the Mickey Mantle #50 selling for $150. The rest of the 1953 Topps cards were worth around $500.

So with about $7,500-worth of the mintest baseball cards I had ever looked at before me, I asked the officer if he would sell me the box full for $150, since I had paid one hell of a big price for his Mantle card.

He slowly reached into the box and pulled out 100 or so of the low-numbered 1952 Topps cards before he sold me the rest. As he stacked them on the table, he said, "I'll probably sell you these soon, but for now, you've bought all you're going to buy."

I tried to buy the rest of the cards for almost six months. I needed them to complete my dream set of mint 1952 Topps Gum cards. When I would call, the captain would always stall me off with "Later." I guess he had kept a small part of his youth in the box that he had sold me 99% of, and he would never part with it.

Not too long after I bought these sets, Topps cards,

along with the rest of the post-war baseball cards, did a big flip-flop backwards in price. Most dealers place the blame on the over-priced 1952 Mickey Mantle #311 card that had no right, they said, to go from $500 in 1979 to $3,500 for mint by late 1980. Alerted by newspaper and trade magazine stories of Mantle's high price, everybody that was able went up in attics, down in basements, and out in garages to hunt for the $3,500 #311 Mickey Mantle, and then other cards by the millions came out of the woodwork and were thrown on the baseball card market.

Mantle #311 tumbled to $800 in only a few months, and with this severe price break, the entire post-war card market collapsed to a point where the bigger dealers in New York would rather pick up a live rattlesnake than handle a 1952 Topps 407-card set containing the famous #311 to #407 "murderer's row."

Today it would be a miracle to find a live buyer for #311 at a price over $500 to $600.

In 1972 Topps began to sell complete 16-team sets of new cards by the box. This ended forever the upward trend of not only all Topps cards issued since 1972, but had a downward effect on all cards printed since the war.

While all this was happening to post-war baseball cards, all the tens of thousands of older pre-war cards have been escalating daily in value. There is a certain magic attached to an antique baseball card. It may be the quaint names of the hundreds of tobacco companies on the different-sized sets of cards, or it may be the antique baseball uniforms. Whatever it is, millions of dollars changes hands yearly in the never-never world of buying and selling the illusive antique baseball card.

Sets of baseball cards issued prior to 1940 continue to be a blue-chip investment. It seems that boys and men are always turned on by baseball cards, and among the men are those with pockets bulging who will buy at your price.

High-priced baseball cards: Babe Ruth (Leaf), $100; Mickey Mantle (Topps), $700; Willie Mays (Topps), $350; Honus Wagner (T), $19,000 (only 10 known); and Napoleon Lajoie (Goudey), $6,250.

22

THE MAN WHO FELL
IN LOVE WITH
MY BASEBALL CARDS

From the very first day in the baseball bubble gum card business, Nate Ross and I were 50-50 partners. I had drawn a circle around Dixon that took in St. Louis and Madison, Chicago and Rock Island. All of these cities and those in between were going to see a baseball card advertising blitz for the following six months.

Our advertising started first in newspapers in St. Louis, Peoria, Bloomington, and Springfield. By advertising in sections, we could run down the cards better, we thought. Nothing came out of these towns except for Peoria, which was always a great baseball town. Peoria brought several thousand good cards into our hands, including a complete set of 1953 Topps Bubble Gum cards with a mint #244 Willie Mays worth $500, and a mint #50 Mickey Mantle worth $150, plus a lot of good, high numbers that put us on our way to complete our first 1952 Topps set, at the time booking for $10,000. We were short only the Mickey Mantle #311 $3,000 card, the #400 Bill Dickey $400 card, and the last card in the 407-card set, Ed Mathews, booking at $750. We were to fill two complete sets of 1952 Topps cards as we bought over 250,000 baseball cards in the six-month period.

The Rockford **Register-Star** brought us three Mickey Mantles, and the Chicago **Tribune** brought us three more. The Dixon **Evening Telegraph** brought one more to our collection out of Polo, plus a complete mint run of the fabled 1952 Topps.

A farmwife had read my ad in the Dixon paper saying I loved Mickey Mantle and would pay $1,000 (at that time) for his #311 card. She told me on the phone that while her husband was out plowing, she went up to the attic to see if she could find this card. She almost fell over, she told me, when she found the #311 with Mickey Mantle holding a bat over his shoulder and ready to swing away.

I drove 75 miles an hour to the farm north of Polo. When I had dodged two big dogs and walked into the kitchen, I saw on the table a half bushel of neatly bundled early 1950 to 1957 cards. I was shown Mantle #311, but it was in only good condition.

However, it didn't take me long to flip through just a few of the thousands of fine cards there to know that I had just hit our first set of 1952 Topps baseball bubble gum cards, among the most valuable in existence. There was also a group of great "star" cards that were also worth some serious money, but I didn't know how much to offer.

"Fifteen hundred for the basketful and Mickey

#311," I ventured.

The farm wife said she had better wait until her husband came in from plowing so I could buy from him. I knew this was not apt to work out with a card-owner because they can see all their childhood in their cards, and to get them away is like pulling teeth. I had to think fast because it was getting towards the supper hour and I knew her husband would be heading in.

I named a figure and threw down on the kitchen table a wad of bills big enough to choke a cow. I suspected the farmer's wife, who was living in a frame house needing work inside and out, hadn't seen that much money in her farming life before. She said, "I don't know what Chuck is going to say about my selling his cards, but go ahead and take them."

I excused myself to go look at some more baseball cards, I said, but instead fairly flew home, where I quickly carried the basket of cards to the basement and locked them up. I didn't want to take any chance of an irate baseball-card-addict husband pulling up screaming bloody murder, with the cards still in my car.

In one swoop, we had bagged many times the amount of valuable cards that we had ever dreamed of finding. Nate took the thousands of dollars worth of mint "star" cards and the sets to his home to sort and price them. All of the star cards, which were worth into three digits, were separated out and kept in his big safe. Nate kept a mint #311 Mantle and a mint #244 Mays standing in a large glass showcase along with his wife's finest antique dishes so he could ogle them every time he'd pass by. Mantle and Mays were his favorite ball players when he was a kid, and from the way he talked about them, he was still nuts about them. He would work until after midnight every night sorting cards. I think it brought out the kid in him.

Nate went to great pains to place each star card in a special plastic container. All sets were kept in rows in a fire-proof steel filing box. The cards were cross indexed as to grade and price.

When I'd go over to Nate's place to relax, all he could talk about was baseball cards. I have heard about guys who fall in love with their big $100,000 classic cars or a fancy Las Vegas dancer, but falling in love with baseball cards was just plain nutty, I told Nate. I asked him to let me take them to my house for safe-keeping, since he lived 10 miles in the country where anyone could break in the door and walk away with the results of all our hard work and money.

Nate would become disagreeable as heck each time I would broach this subject. He wanted to riffle through our cards daily and, at a moment's notice, pull out a mint Mays, Mantle, Babe Ruth, or Lou Gehrig.

The only cards I kept were the two most valuable sets of 1952 Topps cards which we were building on. The big haul north of Polo had completed them to within a few numbers of the 407 cards each. We needed only a few more high numbers. The high and high-priced numbers of this hardest Topps set to complete started with Mantle #311 and were all worth at least $100 each, all the way to Mathews #407, which was booked at $750. Numbers 312, 313 and 314 were all $200 to $300 cards, with Willie Mays #350 worth $300 to $400. The high price of these cards was due to their scarcity, and that to the fact that fewer of the high numbers were printed.

One day I called Nate to tell him that a man had

contacted me from north of Byron saying he had 100,000 baseball cards to sell. I told Nate it sounded fishy, and asked him to take his gun and come with me.

In Nate's old truck we drove six miles out Gulch Road from Byron to an old house with small children playing outside. As we pulled up, a man of 35 or 40 with long hair came sauntering out, saying he was the man we were looking for.

Nate told me that since he had the gun, he would go in and look. For an hour or longer he stayed in the house without once sending me a signal. I began to fear the worst for my little buddy with the big mouth and the big gun. All that kept me from going for help was the sight of the five or six little children playing in and out of the house. I figured a guy couldn't be too nutty with a young family like that.

At last I knew Nate had made progress when the children began the hour-long job of hauling all of their father's 100,000 baseball cards out of his upstairs baseball room. They were all dusty, but filed as a good baseball card collector keeps them.

Once all the full boxes were deposited in the van, Nate came out of the house in conversation with the erst-while owner. The latter came close enough for me to see that he was on something and could use some more. This is why he sold a half a truck-load of mint cards, I told myself.

Nate told him goodby, and as we drove off I immediately asked Nate how much he had paid.

"Guess," he said.

"I don't know what you paid, dealing with that nut."

"I gave him what he asked me, $650."

Can you beat a man working all his life to gather and put in sets and boxes 100,000 cards, and then selling them for nearly nothing? I always said that there are some strange ones out there waiting to be plucked, and this was one of them.

After examining the cards at home, we found there were tens of thousands of basketball, football, and jockey cards of the late 70s that were of little value. We boxed up all these cards and shipped them to a Miami, Florida, dealer for $500. That national dealer had a near stroke when 12 good-sized boxes of bubble gum cards arrived. He said he knew there was going to be a lot, but not that many.

We had made a lot of other good buys by then in our five record-shattering months of buying 250,000 baseball cards in the crazy but fun-filled baseball card business.

One Sunday I ran an ad in the One Shot column in the Chicago *Tribune*, which cost $5. I got a call from Coal City, Illinois, from a 45-year-old city commissioner (I later found out) who said he had 10,000 baseball autographs, the largest such collection in the U.S., for sale. He also sent me a picture of nine baseball team posters as they hung framed on his wall which he also had for sale, but was not sure what they were.

I recognized these team pictures as Fatima Cigarette posters, the rarest baseball cards in the world. To get one of these 1913 posters picturing an entire baseball team, it was necessary to send in to the company 40 small team pictures. The posters were printed with "1913" in the lower left-hand corner, and "Pictorial News Service" on the right-hand corner. Teams pictured included the Brooklyn Nationals,

Chicago Nationals, St. Louis Nationals, and New York Americans, with 16 posters to the set.

Fran and I drove to Coal City, and I looked at the baseball autographs. The commissioner told me his price was $25,000, but he might drop down to $10,000.

"How do you know these are real authographs?" I asked. I had no serious interest in this hard-to-authenticate collection. All the while I was eyeing the team posters on the wall, encased in plastic and in their walnut frames. The commissioner told me that an elderly lady had found them in her attic and given them to him. Even a sports editor from a Chicago newspaper who had come to look at the baseball autographs had not been able to identify them.

I knew they were worth a lot of money. The Baseball Hall of Fame had only two of this 16-card set!

I got on the phone to the human encyclopedia of baseball card knowledge, Lou Ipswich, of New York city. I had already contacted him about the cards, and he had told me to try to buy them for him.

"I'm looking at the cards I told you about," I said to Lou. "They say '1913' on one corner and 'Pictorial New Service' on the other. In the middle (I lied) they say 'Fatima Cigarettes'."

"There's no Fatima wording on them," Lou said. I knew then that the posters were for real and nothing phony.

I paid $450 a card for the posters, or $4,050 for some posters that you might give to the paper drive if you had seen them lying on a pile of newspapers.

When I got back to Dixon, I called Lou and told him that I had nailed down nine of the 16 cards in the set, with his favorite team, the Brooklyn Nationals, among them. He was elated, and I made a friend for life, as well as receiving a nice commission.

Later I saw the same posters described in the baseball card magazine I subscribe to, with the information that the biggest antique baseball card dealer in the country, Joe Brokoff, would pay $1,100 each for any 1913 Fatima Cigarette team posters. If my handing nine of them to Lou almost free at around $500 each made him happy, it now made me feel twice as unhappy. I would have collected $9,900 — over twice as much. So it went in the tricky baseball card business, hit one lick and miss two.

Of course Nate received 50% of the commission for just being my partner for those hectic five months when we bought almost one quarter million baseball cards, with over half of them coming from the baseball card fanatic's house near Byron.

We had sold only a few cards to keep up in part with the expenses of advertising in big city and small town newspapers in every direction. By this time our advertising kitty was so empty there was nothing left to advertise with.

I told Nate it was time we disposed of all the cards he had neatly stacked in filing cabinets. He had kept only the best stock, sending all the lower-grade cards down to the Miami dealer.

I wanted to advertise our cards nationally through a trade magazine. But Nate opted for flying out to the big baseball card national convention at the Disneyland Hotel complex in California, which he had seen announced in the monthly *Baseball Card Digest* that we subscribed to. Nate said that was where the big money was, and we would pop the dealer's eyes out with the great amoung of good cards we had.

I finally agreed to let Nate take my half of the

cards along with his to sell at the largest baseball card meet in the nation.

I lost track of Nate and all of our thousands of dollars worth of cards after he took off from O'Hare. I had heard that you could really get ripped off by some of the over 100 professional cards dealers at the convention, and after all my cards were on that jet, I waited and listened for a phone call to let me know how everything was going.

I waited for three or four days before Nate finally called me late at night.

"I'm sick, Dan," he said. "I've gone and got myself low-balled." He talked so low I could just barely hear him.

I asked Nate to explain that "low-balled" meant. He said he had carried all our cards into a big bourse room where all the dealers from around the nation met to show their cards, with thousands of dollars in cash stuffed in their pockets, and they all walked up to see his cards. Nate said he was called a "walk-on" by other dealers because he had just walked in un-announced with cards to sell.

"I walked in," Nate mumbled on, "and then all these dealers converged on me like piranha to clean the meat off an intruder. They all oohed and aahed at our cards," Nate continued, "and convinced me that to get top money we should auction the cards off. I did this with all our cards today, paying out 10% commission, and they all got together and low-balled me."

"What the hell does that mean, 'low-balled'?" I asked again. "I worked for five months and have driven 20,000 miles to buy those cards, and Fran did the driving, while you didn't do anything but sort cards til midnight and longer every night. What the devil is going on out there?"

"I told you they all got together and took turns bidding on our sets and best cards, and then they divided them all up amongst each other after the auction, just like the Persian oriental rug buyers do with the rugs at the Chicago auctions. They ganged up just like they do, and I came out with $6,000 after the comissions. They stole all of the Mickey Mantle −311 cards at $300 each. All of our Bowman sets, 1948 to 1950, which were some of our best cards, they stole."

When Nate came back, it was the end of our card dealing. I lost approximately $9,000 in those six months. Fran and I had put thousands of miles on our car, and I had gone through countless spine-tingling buying sessions.

During that period, we bought every kind of product baseball cards, such as Swift's Meat, Wonder Bread, Coca Cola, Redman Chewing Tobacco, and the comic strip bubble gum cards.

Baseball cards are still going strong today, with two national baseball card magazines issued monthly. In 1980 a new price guide came out, and cards from the 30's to 50's caught even more attention. Hundreds of big baseball card bourses are held across the nation. It is another world at the card meets.

At a recent Sotheby Parke Bernet auction where rare baseball cards were featured, a 1913 T-206 Pittsburgh Honus Wagner tobacco card sold for $25,000. There are only nine or ten known of these rarest of all cards.

If this doesn't convince you that baseball bubble gum cards are a big, big business, then I have wasted this story. One thing to remember, if you decide to go into this business, don't take a partner.

23

THE UNIQUE
BASEMENT COUNTRY
STORE HOBBY

In the early 1960's, I bought a large and beautiful tin DeLaval cream separator sign that got me started in the wonderful field of buying and selling old advertising signs and old country store items. I paid very little for the DeLaval sign, but believe you me, I sold it for $575 to a restaurant owner. You can see from this figure that good advertising signs, preferably the tin ones, are not cheap. Today the same three foot by two foot sign retails for $1,200 and is going higher every day.

The reason old signs and country store fixtures are so high is because the more affluent are often transforming their basements into simulated 1890's country stores complete with wood counters, brass cash registers, and shelves filled with tin containers.

The country store collectors I know are husband

and wife teams, with the women doing a lot of the bidding at auctions. I have been made a believer by how
determined they are if they decide an item is right for
their "store."

This past year I watched in Monroe, Wisconsin,
as the Christianson Old Country Store 40-year collection of advertising signs and turn-of-the-century store
fixtures were sold at three separate sales. I saw one
tin sign after another selling from $1,000 for a large
farm wagon builder's sign to over $2,500 for a big
round tin Bull Durham sign.

Thirty six-drawer spool cabinets were sold for
around $700 each at one of these sales. I have bought
many in the 60's for $5 and sold them for $15. Today
most of the walnut six-drawer and eight-drawer spool
cabinets are made into beautiful end tables.

Bidders came from every state in the union, and
their desire to buy at the country store auctions was
almost maniacal. I watched a 1900 German counter
cigar lighter sell for $3,600. A 10″ tall paper Bull
Durham sign showing Blacks sold for $800. An old
Budweiser beer tray went for $900.

I saw several head-high two-wheel cast iron Enter-
prise coffee grinders sell for $750 + . Small tin tobac-
co containers didn't take a back seat either. Several
10″ tall pear-shaped Roly Poly tins sold for $600 each.
The rare Scotland Yard Roly Poly tin, which I had sold
before the country store craze hit for $100, brought
$1,000 from a West Coast dealer.

A tobacco tin with the name Dixie Kid sold for
$300. At the turn of the century, when the tobacco con-
tents was emptied from these tins, they were often
used for lunch buckets. What made the tin fetch so
much was the embossed pictured on it of a Black boy

lying on a fleecy cloud. Also, it was mint. ("Mint" to members of the container collecting clubs of America means it is worth double the book price.)

I have barely touched on the big collecting field of old store items that is well entrenched around the country. During the past five years or so, whenever I advertise fine old signs, be they cardboard, tin, or glass, the response is always heavy. A case in point is the two glass Woolworth signs that I recently sold for $300 each. They read, "Nothing in this store over 10 Cts." and underneath, the "Woolworth" lettering.

There is just a lot of money out there in Traderland waiting to buy old signs and tins at almost any price. The price is not important to most collectors. It is finding and then buying the desired country store item.

Once the country store collectors have turned their basement into well-equipped general stores, they usually do most of their entertaining there. I can imagine how much fun it must be to dine from old wire, heart-backed ice cream chairs around marble-topped ice cream tables, with quaint advertising signs on the walls. When a cocktail is needed, the country store counter is a convenient place to order from.

So keep a sharp look-out for old advertising signs, preferably in tin, but also in paperboard. The tin signs, if tobacco or whiskey is advertised on them, may sell for $400 up to $1,200, while good paperboard signs bring about one third of that price.

Your best bet for these signs is to zero in on antique sales in small towns. I have bid on and bought hundreds of these signs over the past 25 years, and have nearly always doubled my money and sometimes more.

If I get lonesome for the signs I've sold, I can look

at them on the walls of many of the antique-decor restaurants and bars in northern Illinois.

Besides signs, country store fixtures are always in demand by the country store collector. Old display cases are good sellers, as well as the oak or walnut six-drawer spool cabinets.

The best bets are tin advertising signs and tin containers. If you see them at an auction, don't drop out of the bidding. I predict the country store hobby will continue to grow over the next year or two.

An advertising sign common in the early 1900's, worth $400-$500 today.

24

WHO WAS ARTIST F. M. KRUSEMAN?
— WORTH $42,000
TO A LUCKY YOUNG DEALER

In the summer of 1980, I was looking through the Rockford paper's auction section when I saw that a good sale was coming up the next Saturday, with more old walnut furniture and dishes than I had seen advertised all year. I cut the ad out and stuck it on the kitchen wall along with other auction announcements.

That night I called Nate Ross, one of my two antique pupils, and told him of the good sale coming up. When I had taken Nate as an antique student some time before, all he had was a strong desire to absorb the know-how I had acquired the hard way. For my part, I felt I had a lot of knowledge to transmit and no one to give it to, because none of my four children give a darn for antiques, which came from growing up in a house where they were always warned "Don't bump this," or "Don't touch that."

I cautioned Nate that if he was going to be a student of mine, it would take me ten years to graduate him so that he could go out and buy antiques on his own and make money with them.

Our favorite auction firm of Roy Stenzel and Bert Nichols was going to be conducting the Saturday sale, I told Nate. He said he would be there. In the meantime, unknown to me, Nate drove to Rockford on Friday night for a sneak preview. Roy always warned people at his sales not to attempt to do this. The sellers would have been told to bolt the door on early lookers, who will try to buy fine items cheap ahead of the sale. But Nate is a persuasive little guy, and he got into the house where all the sale goodies were sitting around.

Nate told me nothing about this preview until the next morning, when I called and asked if he was ready to drive up to the sale. It was raining heavily with a dark sky everywhere we looked and Nate didn't think he'd go, because the only items of interest up there were two rather nice oil paintings. The rest was all common. The sale might be called off anyway because of the weather.

"Stenzel never cancels a sale," I told Nate. "If the paintings are good, you'd better drive up in your truck and buy them." I could do a lot of persuading, too.

Nate finally said yes, and when Fran and I got to the sale, we saw Nate's old white truck already parked. We soon spotted the two oil paintings leaning against a tree. It was raining hard by then, 10:30 a.m., which was sale time. It was a good thing Roy carried a lot of plastic sheets for this contingency. The oils were covered as well as everything else, and it was impossible to get even a small look at them.

The auctioneers moved the sale along fast, putting

out a lot of the common goods in boxes and selling it that way. Then it was the turn of the paintings. Roy walked down by the tree where they were leaning in their big 1840-50 gilt frames. Nate seemed to be the only serious bidder, and he got them for $105 apiece. The frames were worth almost that much.

Nate had bought the paintings without even knowing who the artist was. I can still see him running in the rain, carrying first one, then the other, big, heavy framed paintings to his truck a half block away.

Nate hung the pictures side by side in his living room and called me to come and see them. I was disappointed as I didn't care for the paintings. They were landscapes called "Summer" and "Winter". The summer scene showed meadows and leafy trees with a small house nestled by a lake. But the scenes were too desolate-looking for me. Nate pointed out the artist's name, F. M. Kruseman. Neither one of us had ever heard of him before. I left, and was not to see the paintings again until the spring of 1982, because I went my way and Nate went his, starting to do things other than antique dealing.

In the interval, I learned from Nate's wife, Joni, that they had offered the paintings to various antique dealers for $1,200, but there had been no takers. Then they had almost sold them to a rug dealer who had been to their home to pick up some oriental rugs, and had offered them $1,150. The dealer said he knew nothing about art or artists, but was gambling on their making some money at a rug auction he periodically held.

Thinking this was a good price, Nate had asked Joni if it was OK with her to sell them, but Joni, who is an artist in her own right, asked Nate not to sell the paintings, because she had grown fond of them.

In the meantime, Nate had gotten sick of the paintings and in fact had not cared for them after I told him I didn't like them. Every time he looked at their big gilt frames, he wanted to get rid of them.

Later that year Nate went to the library and found that F. M. Kruseman was a 19th Century Flemish artist, which did not tell him very much.

At Christmastime that year, I gave Joni and Nate a subscription to *Antiques* magazine which frequently pictures great antique works of art offered for sale. A few months later, Nate excitedly called me to say that Joni had noticed an F. M. Kruseman painting advertising in the magazine by a New York dealer. The painting was pictured in a full-page color spread! I couldn't believe it without seeing it so Nate brought the magazine down to show me, and suggested we call the New York dealer to find out the price. Using a made-up name, we called and learned the price was $50,000. I thought Nate would never stop laughing when he heard this news.

At that moment, a plan to sell the Krusemans was set in motion. We made a call at my suggestion to the Sotheby auction galleries in New York city to find out how the Krusemans could be auctioned. The call got prompt attention from the head of the art depatment. Nate was asked to send good close-up photos and any pertinent information. Later he received a call telling him to send the paintings in wooden crates made at a Chicago shop. By then Nate was not trusting anyone with his Krusemans, so he got his brother to go with him to deliver the paintings in person. They held them on their laps on the plane all the way to New York.

Then Nate ran into more expense, which was $600

to have the paintings pictured in color in a Sotheby auction catalogue. They would appear along with other paintings to be sold at the next month's sale. The paintings would be numbered in the order of their sale, with their estimated value or expected selling price listed.

When the catalogue arrived, it pegged "Winter" at $25,000 and "Summer" at $18,000. The tension before the sale, both at my house and at Nate's modest home where he lived with Joni and their four children, was high. The week of the sale Nate and Joni flew to New York city, and anticipating their profit, stayed at the Waldorf-Astoria for $160 a day and had lobster dinner sent up to their room.

As the sale began, Nate and Joni were in the gallery. When the painting ahead of his sold for $185,000, Nate became ecstatic. He envisioned a like price. But he had been careful to place a buy-back bid of $15,000 on each painting, in case they should not be bid up that high.

The time for the auction of Lot 121, "Winter", by F. M. Kruseman, owned by Mr. and Mrs. Nate Ross, of Sterling, Illinois, finally came and the painting was placed on a big easel. It was a good bidding audience. However, the bids on "Winter" were not what Nate hoped. They finally inched over the $15,000 protective bid and climbed to $18,500. Nate and Joni were both disappointed. In fact Nate almost bought it back, thinking he might sell it for more by advertising it in *Antiques* magazine.

The next painting to be placed on the easel was "Summer," which suffered it way up to $12,750 and so remained unsold. Nate and Joni left the gallery at once and headed for home, giving instructions to an oriental rug dealer friend who was staying longer to pick up the painting and take it to his rug gallery in Chicago, where they would get it later. Earlier, of course, Nate had had the paintings insured.

The next I heard about "Summer" was Nate's report that the rug dealer had called from New York and told him that during an argument with airplane attendants about taking the painting aboard. It had been caught in a strong air current and went tumbling down the runway, where the canvas was ripped! The dealer offered to reimburse Nate for half the price of the painting. Nate told him to forget it, since the painting was insured, but to get the pieces back to him as soon as possible.

It took a year to get the insurance check for the painting, which was for $9,000. In the meantime, Nate had paid $100 to have the painting professionally repaired in Chicago. He then sent it back to the Sotheby galleries for another try at the roses. And the roses were there, because this time, even though the painting had had major repair, it brought a bigger price than the first time, $14,500!

One of the most amazing antique stories I have ever come across is how this young salesman of modest means turned an ordinary-looking pair of oil paintings purchased for $210 into $42,000. I urge readers to be on the look-out for just such good oil paintings at garage sales and auctions, where often people do not know what they put out.

Nate told me that if he did well on the sale of his Krusemans, he would take me to Europe for six weeks that summer. I haven't even been taken on a trip to Rockford for dinner yet. I am still waiting.

25

THE
PAPER GOODS
CHASE

Old magazines used to be advertised at nearly every house or farm sale, sometimes by the bale and sometimes by the hay rack full. Once in 1966 at a Lake Geneva, Wisconsin sale, I came across an extensive collection of pre-1930 magazines. I picked that accumulation apart with pin-point selection of the best--the 1920 to 1928 **Ladies Home Journals** with their Rose O'Neill Kewpie pages, the 1911 and 1918 **Journals** with their Betty Bonnet doll cut-outs, and the 1920 to early 1930s **Pictorial Reviews** with their Dolly Dingle cut-out pages.

It was at this auction that I made Harriet "Flint-face" Frazer whimper and hit for home crying because I would not share the loot with her.

I did a brisk business in those days in the magazine paper doll business, mainly to the West coast. Girls from seven to 70 loved the many life-like doll cut-outs in magazines. There were some big collectors then of magazine cut-outs with even bigger pocketbooks.

I used to sell the Betty Bonnet doll pages with the complete magazine for $4 or $5. Kewpies were red-hot best-sellers all through the 1960s. Nothing could touch them for lady buyers' demand. I ended up selling my last **Ladies Home Journals** with their darling, precious Kewpies at play and Kewpies at Christmas for $7 apiece, and there was only one Kewpie page to each issue. The magazines were of no value to anyone then except for those pages. When I found **Pictorial Reviews** with their Dolly Dingles, all I had to do was call a customer in San Francisco, who would snap them all up for $5 a copy.

Now you can see why Harriet "Flintface" Frazer asked me to share the long runs of ladies' and men's magazines with her by first my bidding on and buying a group and then her doing the same. I told Harriet what I had once been told, "This is an auction, isn't it? If you want to buy, then bid." It was then that she turned away saying, "You never give another dealer a chance," and ran to her car genuinely crying, because nearly every magazine in that big collection was a sure $5 bill.

Another big magazine seller then was the **Saturday Evening Post**. In 1965, when I was deep into the papergoods business, I got a call from a Rockford lady who said she had some **Posts** for sale. When we reached the address, I was led to two empty upstairs bedrooms and found the floors covered with complete runs of 1900 to 1956 mint **Posts**. The charming old lady who was offering them for sale had saved every issue, as her folks had done before her, and they were all neatly tied in bundles of 12. I looked down at a potential $2,000 to $3,000 when I asked the seller how much she wanted for them.

"They cost us five cents each when we bought them, and I think I should get at least twice as much for them now," she said. I hemmed and hawed and agreed, keeping back my delight at the ten cent price for perhaps 1,000 mint issues, and called Fran out of the car where she always waits for me.

With a fast count, we came up with 66 bundles of *Posts*, or 792 magazines, which added up to $79.20 for the gracious lady. She had planned to give them all to her next block paper drive, she said, to make room for a new bedroom suite.

It seemed we had to go up and down a flight of rickety steps forever to load the heavy bundles into our car. I was so darned anxious to get loaded, I fell down a section of the steps on my head.

Once we were on our way home, I asked Fran, "Do you know how much money is back there?"

She didn't know, nor did she care. All she said was, "I'll know when I see the money."

"There are at least 140 Norman Rockwell covers back there at $5 each," I said, "which is $700, and at least 250 1920's and 30's magazines with black and white and color classic car ads at $3 each, that's $750, and after I sell the car ads, I can buy the magazine back and resell it for $1. I know there is at least $2,000 to $2,500 worth of magazines back there."

There was a lot of money in pre-1930 magazines then, not only for the car ads and doll cut-outs, but for features such as the beautifully colored Maxfield Parrish prints, that were always good for $7.50, and *Ladies' Home Journal* Maxfield Parrish centerfolds advertising Mazda lights.

Today all of these magazines for pre-1930 years are worth from $3 to $10 each: *Vanity Fair, Pictorial Review, Delineator, Saturday Evening Post, Theatre Magazine,* and *Woman's Home Companion*. Colored showroom brochures and car manuals of the 1920's are worth up to $50 each for classic cars and $20 for average cars. All pre-1934 Coca-Cola magazine advertising is worth good money. The best ads are pre-1914. I just sold for $300 a Coke ad covering front and back covers of a 1914 *American Boy*. Don't tear these ads out of magazines! Send the whole magazine to buyers.

The Godey's and Peterson's *Ladies' Books* from 1840 to 1875 are worth from $50 to $75 each if they have their around 12 colored French fashion plates intact. With even one missing, your book will lose one third of its value. If all are gone, a realistic price is $15.

The pulp magazines, selling for five cents during the Depression, are today some of the highest valued magazines ever published. There are great many pulps to look for at garage sales and auctions, such as *G-8, Shadow, Spider, Horror, Argosy, Blue Book, Weird Tales, Dime Mystery,* etc. Most of the 1930's pulps sell for $5 to $100 per copy. Buy an *Antique Trader* and scan their Books Wanted to Buy classified section for a check on all the 1930's and earlier pulps and magazines in demand. There are books, as well, that are highly sought after, and there is a good bundle of money waiting if you can locate early books on Indians, the West, Mormons, and pre-1900 medical books, just to mention a few.

Hunting for paper goods in past years was like searching for paper money or going to Las Vegas. You never could tell at what sale you might hit the old magazine jackpot.

Nowadays, the chance of locating the quantity and quality of magazines that I describe in this article is next to nil. Most are in museums or private collections, having been bought from dealers like myself.

All I have to remember my paper goods chase by is the fine home and life it helped give my wife and myself. I can honestly say that chasing down fine magazines packed more thrills into my antique career than any other phase of it. The excitement of hitting a big magazine jackpot in attic or basement made the long days and years of my paper goods chase well worthwhile.

Paper dolls bring $15 a page, Betty Bonnet from "Ladies' Home Journal" and Dolly Dingle from 1924 "Pictorial Review."

High-priced comics: Superman 1939 No. 1, $2,750; Batman 1940 No. 4, $2,000; Action 1938 No. 1, $7,000; Whiz 1940 No. 2, $4,500; Marvel 1979 No. 1, $9,300.

26

THE CHICAGO
ORIENTAL RUG
GANG EXPOSE'

In the early 1960's, oriental rugs at sales were a common sight. Who would want an oriental rug in the house? Hadn't we just gone through a hellish war with Orientals? Anything oriental was bad medicine to the antique sale goer.

This is when I got my start. Once, in 1966, I paid $175 for a beautiful scenic carpet that had been advertised in Rockford incorrectly as an American machine-made oriental. All the other antique dealers at the sale passed it up. After holding it a few years, I sold it at auction for $8,300.

This is to point out that it is hard even for auctioneers and dealers to distinguish a machine-made oriental from a genuine hand-made one.

The first thing to do is turn over the corner and see if there is a label which will tell you that the rug is American and machine-made, in which case it will be of no value in the oriental rug market.

The next test is to bring the rug's back-side up close to your eyes and look along the long row of knots for a weaving imperfection, a slight curve of the knots. If you see this, you know the rug was woven by hand, because a weaving machine does not vary its knots nor does it put a small bend in its rows of knots.

Oriental, or Persian, rug weaving progresses from each end of the rug to the middle. On the big carpets, as many as five weavers would be working at each end, weaving toward the center with all their intricate and beautiful designs and colors. Some rugs might take years to complete. Finely woven Keshans and silks in the old days were always woven by children, whose small fingers alone were nimble enough to tie the million tight knots.

My business at the outset was with a rug advertiser of long standing in the magazine **Antiques** that I used to read every month at the library. I sent a letter to his Syracuse, New York, address one day telling him that I had just bought two big orientals and some smaller sizes, and asking if he would be interested in them. He sent me back a letter saying he would send me a long, round rug container for each rug, and that after he had looked them over, he would call and give me his best price for them.

I was so anxious to get the rugs to him so I could see some money that I tied them in rolls and sent them Railway Express without even a wrapper. I guess if something is superior, it doesn't need a wrapper, as the owner of the prestigious rug company called and told me the rugs were very good and he would like to buy them. That began the many years of his buying all the good rugs I could locate within the 100-mile circumference of Dixon.

Then in 1968 I met Mike and Sid Kermenian, Iranian rug buyers from Chicago. From that day until 1976, these two Iranians were my outlet for oriental rugs. I was their buyer in this big area, managing to buy all the biggest and rarest rugs to surface in it. Among my buys were a 24-foot mint Kerman rug with ten smaller prayer rugs woven into it, a rug that I sold to the Kermenian brothers in those poorer days for $4,500.

I bought a rare double eagle Kazak throw rug, plus a six by nine foot Kazak in soft burnt oranges and pinks described in another story. The latter two were, without doubt, the two greatest rugs I ever sold the Kermenians. I could kick myself for not keeping the rare mint circa 1840 double eagle Kazak, for had I kept it, I could pick up the phone today, and this throw rug with the claw-like fingers woven into it would find a new home for $6,500.

In my dealings with the Kermenians, I learned that their father had previously owned a Tehran rug mall booth in the downtown area where all the oriental rug trading formerly took place. When the Shah was booted out, the Ayatollah made it tough to make money in any way, reaching his slimy hand into the dealers' pockets, asking for more and more money to allow them to operate. Mike and Sid's dad sold his 75 by 30 foot booth just in time to get out of the country, but got little of the money he was paid for it. Today he is the oriental rug boss of Chicago.

When I went to Iran to learn more about how rugs are made and sold, I swore I was back in the time of Christ. Donkeys were being pulled along by women in black dresses and veils, with their men riding on them. One day I was standing in the center of the very bustling town of Tehran, hearing automobile traffic whizzing by, when a long camel train came out of the Middle Ages, it seemed, winding its way into the downtown area at the five o'clock rush hour. I think I must have shaken my head and rubbed my eyes. The camels were carrying huge bundles of oriental rugs. There were over 100 camels bound for the rug mall where the Kermenians were to move out hurriedly in 1975.

I learned that these rugs had already been bought and paid for by the Tehran rug dealers. Tehran was the rug-trading capital of the world then, with 95% of the rugs finding their way either to the U.S. or the huge German oriental rug market. I watched, stupified, as the procession loaded with rugs from the far northern and western provinces moved past me. Just when the lead camel driver stopped for a stop light, I saw an affluent-looking American woman rush out from near where I was standing and began bargaining with him to buy some of the rugs. She yelled louder and louder, "I want to buy your rugs," and finally when she pulled a big wad of American cash out of her pocketbook, the camel driver began to give her some serious looks and attention. Then, believe it or not, with traffic already backed up, the lead camel went down on his knees and then his rear, and with this, all of the camels in the long train lay down one after the other until they were all comfortably resting on the busiest street in downtown Tehran. The traffic jam was unbelievable, while those two nuts bargained for rugs in the middle of the street. Within a few minutes, the Tehran police were there and got the caravan started once more on its way to the downtown rug mall.

The rug business went sour for me as soon as an over-supply of Iranian rug buyers hit this country in 1974. I decided to concentrate on Mettlach and Royal Doulton. However, I kept my fingers in the pie by every once in a while plucking an oriental rug-plum out from under the Iranian Mafia's noses. They had their oriental rug spotters and buyers spread out like a web all across my former rug dominion. Where I had ruled for over a decade, I now had been usurped by the "black people," as they are known in Chicago sales. You cannot bid against an Iranian at a sale, or he will bury you. The Iranian rug buyers cut their teeth on rugs, and by the time they are eight or nine years old, they know their rugs into the hundreds of different names and grades.

These Iranian rug buyers are a breed of their own, and they are both sensitive and ruthless. They are sensitive in dealing with their parents, kind and loving to their wives and children, but when a good rug is involved, they will cut your hands off to take it away from you. They are also good actors, and can get down on their knees and cry and beg for mercy to close a rug deal in their favor, which they have done with me.

Not one rug has ever been bought for a good re-sale profit by a non-Iranian where they have been in attendance. They believe in freezing you out even if it costs them a huge over-bid to do it. This is done to teach all encroachers on their territory to stay out. Now that local rug dealers have found how determined what we call the "Chicago Mafia" is to stamp out competition, they do not go to sales where they might run across an Iranian buyer.

At sales where the Iranians are out in force, one of their leaders does all the bidding on the rugs. As soon as the sale of rugs is over, they gather around him and conduct a split of the money the rug would have cost normally, above what was paid at the auction. If a rug brought $3,500, for example, as one did last week at a sale I attended, and the "Mafia" rug chieftain bid it in, and it was actually a mint Keshan that could have been expected to bring $8,500, then there would be a split made of the money above what it was bought for, or $5,000. If there were six Iranian buyers laying off, then they would all receive an equal share of the $5,000 which they cheated the estate out of. In other words, if you were standing idly by while I bought an $8,500 rug for $3,500, you wouldn't have done this for nothing.

I was told many times that the reason there were so many tens of thousands of young Iranian rug buyers in this country was to buy good oriental rugs for the Shah. He had financed their passage for the purpose of sending these rugs back for his private collection. I was told that when he hurriedly left the country, his rug collection was worth several billion dollars, and now is being liquidated by the Ayatollah to pay Iranian bills.

This dumping of the Shah's billion dollar collection of fine Sarouks, Kermans, Keshans, and silks onto the U.S. market has deflated it so much that many of the 20,000 Park Avenue oriental rug dealers have been forced out of business. There is an over-supply mainly of the Sarouk-type of rug. To make the situation worse, the Germans are not buying as usual, due to a severe Depression there.

The Germans for over a decade were the only

foreign buyers of what fine oriential rugs could be located in this country and exported. Germans love oriental rugs. Almost every German house has wall to wall oriental rugs, with others hung on the wall or used as table covers.

Since the Shah's rugs were put on the market to pay Iraqi war bills, there has been a noticeable softness in the New York city rug market. No longer are just average oriental rugs in demand, but only the best. Those with even a small amount of wear are not wanted, which is a big change-over from just a few years ago. Then a rug could be worn down to the warp with very little knap left, and would sell for decent money. No more.

So walk away from an oriental rug that isn't near mint. Rug buyers would just as soon pay double for a mint rug. There is always plenty of serious money around the country to buy mint anything in any antique field. I have found this to be true all through my antique career. The rich investor will buy at your price anything that is old, beautiful, and in fine condition. This premium paid for an antique is the price due for someone caring enough for a thing of beauty to keep it perfect for one, two, or three hundred years.

The Old Coot with part of his collection. Illinois sets (1909-1983) run $400-$600.

27

THE OLD LICENSE PLATE COLLECTOR WHO DIED WITH HIS LICENSE PLATES ON -- THE WALL

Automobile license plate collecting is a big hobby around the country. It always has been since collectors started in 1909, when the first Illinois license plates were made, by tacking them up inside their garage walls. Every year when the new set would be put on the car, the old set would get nailed up.

Locating these old collectors has enabled me to buy four or five complete runs of Illinois license plates, 1909 to 1950. Plates after 1939 are not worth collecting because they are too plentiful.

The early license plate runs are not usually broken up when located by dealers or collectors. A fine run will command a $750 price tag today, especially if four-digit plates like one of the runs I bought at a sale in 1964. The amazing thing about this set was that the plates bore the same four digits all the way through.

Along with this set, I bought a set of round aluminum state of Illinois "bicycle" tags that formerly were affixed around the steering wheel or on the dash by a car-plate owner. The so-called bicycle tax was levied when a lot of bicycles used city streets and state roads, and when the car came into use on the same roads, the term stayed "bicycle tax." These two-inch medallions were sold for nine years only up until 1918.

In the 50's and 60's I'd usually find a few bicycle tags at estate sales, and would sell them for $2 and $3. Today they sell for $10, and there is a big group of automobile club members who want a certain year to match the year of the antique car they drive.

Every time I'd find a complete set in those days I'd call an Iowa man who was both a collector and dealer in plates from all over the country. I would ask $300 then for a complete run, 1909 to 1950, if near mint. He didn't buy rusted or bent plates at all.

The first Illinois license plate was made of wood and zinc and was hung on a car with a pair of leather straps.

Today there are rare, rusted plates that can sell for more than mint ones did in the 60's. I just sold last month a run of rusty 1917 to 1936 Illinois license plates pairs for $175. Just 15 years ago, I couldn't have gotten much more than $50 for them.

The porcelain Pennsylvania auto license plates from the early 1900's sell for $100 to $200 today for only one year of plates. They are among the most expensive of all car plates today. I have looked for a set of these porcelain plates for over 30 years but none has ever crossed my path.

The single pairs of Illinois license plates which I used to buy, I would sell mostly to license plate dealers who refurbished antique cars for their main living. The best prices I received were for 1909 to 1939 plates, which were the years of the big, good-looking and very expensive Cords, Cadillacs, Pierce-Arrows, Lincolns, and Packards. The owners of these cars had a lot of money tied up in them, and would think nothing of paying me $50 for a mint pair of 1924 plates to go on their $20,000 to $50,000 pink cabriolet Lincoln Continental or Cadillac town car.

There is, all of a sudden, an even bigger demand for pre-1940 motorcycle license plates than for car plates. The motorcycle plates carry an automatic price tag of $50. They are sometimes found at country and garage sales along with the car license plates and aluminum bicycle tags that we have discussed.

Back in 1965, when I was chasing down license plates with wanted-to-buy-old-license-plates ads in many of our area papers, I heard the report that a man around Princeton, Illinois, owned over 10,000 fine old license plates from across the nation. I am a guy that people had better not tell things like that to, because I love to hunt--both wild game and antiques--especially when you are talking $10 each plate. That, times 10,000 plates, would be a cool $100,000. (I've heard of robbing banks for one tenth this amount and risking getting shot.)

The hunt for this dream collection began in early summer. I remember it well, because it was then that Fran, my wife, presented me with Linda, my youngest girl. I did nothing in my spare time for almost the next three months but question farmers near Princeton to see if they had heard of the license plate collector. All would shake their heads. I also questioned several antique dealers in the Princeton area, and they, too, answered no.

It was getting toward late fall when I told Fran it would be fun to go down to see her dad near Florid, about 60 miles away, with our new baby daughter and the three other children.

Fran agreed to the Sunday drive. As we passed through the south edge of Princeton, six miles from Florid, I saw an old codger in blue overalls, work jacket and an old hat, leaning up against the side of his barn. For some reason known only to God, I had never come to this vicinity in my search for the 10,000 license plates. I pulled a few feet into the driveway to the barn, and as I got out, I told Fran to move over into the driver's seat in case I'd have to exit the place fast. I told Fran to keep the engine idling, because this guy with his holey overalls looked nutty enough to be living on a gold mine of early license plates, and he could be nutty in other ways.

I introduced myself as an antique collector (never a dealer) and asked the old codger if he had anything in the barn to sell. He took me into the barn but with a high-pitched, squeaky voice told me that an antique dealer had cleaned out all his oak furniture and horse-drawn farm machinery the year before. As I kept searching around for a clue as to whether this might be the man who owned the license plate collection, the old codger ended my quest. Peering through thick-lensed glasses too small for his round face, he asked, "Would you like to see my license plate collection."

My heart skipped a beat as he led me to his large farm house with shades all pulled down. As I walked into the big front room and adjusted my eyes to the darkness, I nearly fell over, because the walls and even the ceilings were all covered with rare, early license plates from every state in the union.

I followed the old man into one room after the other, and everywhere it was the same. He pointed out rare porcelain plates on the ceiling as we walked.

Then as we entered the kitchen toward the back of the house, I noted an old lady feeding what appeared to be 100 to 150 cats. They were eating out of tin cans and off of plates on the floor and on the kitchen counters. It was now beginning to look like I had walked into a mad house, and I began to want out fast.

The old codger introduced me to the old lady, who was, as it turned out, his unmarried sister. He told me he had stayed single too, hoping sis would get married first, but since she didn't, he stayed single, too, to take care of her. I guess this is the custom in some ethnic groups.

It was a sad story to hear, and for some reason, it was even sadder to see all those rooms, even to closets and bath rooms, studded with license plates. I could easily see there were at least 10,000 in the ten-room house. But I was becoming more frightened with every moment of being in the eerie place, with the Old Coot asking me squeakily every minute, "How do you like my license plates?" or "What do you think of that pair?"

I had already felt the Old Coot out on whether I could buy his collection, and was told, "Not right today." I was still hopeful of buying something, like the other dealer had in getting the oak furniture. I was starting to edge backward towards the front door when I saw another room that had not been opened yet. I thought to myself, there just might be some great and valuable antique in there.

I edged back a bit more, and then sideways, with

the scads of cats seeming to follow me as I moved toward the mysterious door. I thought I would try to sneak a look if possible, and I had turned the knob and opened the door just slightly when a big wave of moving and surging power pushed the door wide and into my startled face. I was practically run over and under by what looked like 1,000 more mean, vicious, clawing, tearing, squalling tom cats who had (I was later told by Coot) been segregated because they were troublesome to the quieter cats.

The battle between the once-peaceful cats and the troublesome cats erupted all over the house with the yowls and spitting as of caged tigers. The Old Coot began swinging a kitchen broom around and around, all the time glancing at me as if he was going to pull a gun and shoot me.

I saw a clearing to the door in between the hundreds of cat fights, through which I exited in less time than it takes to say "scat cat", and I know that I shattered my old 9.9 track record in the 100-yard dash at Dixon High School as I made it to the car. Fran took off with a big burst of speed, smoking up the back tires to make our get-away.

As I told Fran about the episode, I added, "I will never go back to that cat house again."

However, I went back one winter ten years later. I saw nothing around the place to indicate that any one lived there any longer. But as I walked closer to the house, I smelled wood smoke and saw a freshly-stacked pile of wood. I thought I might still get a crack at the license plates after all.

I knocked on the old kitchen door, and was asked in to unbelieveable squalor. I looked at a much-older Old Coot sitting stooped over next to his cast iron cook stove, the only source of heat. I looked all around the kitchen and saw no cats. His sister had died since I had been there, and now all was quiet in the license-papered rooms. Nothing else had changed, the rare Pennsylvania porcelains were still on the ceiling. Papers were stacked all over the floor and it stank to high heaven in the filthy rooms.

With a sad heart--and a much fatter pocketbook than I had the last time I was there--I walked over to a weakened Coot and asked him if he would sell his license plate collection. His answer came out clearly in the same squeaky voice, "No, I think I'll keep them a while longer. I don't know what I'd do without my plates. I couldn't live without them."

I thanked him and left. I felt it wouldn't be long before Coot would be exiting his house feet first. Then a big marble slab ought to be erected, I thought, from some of the proceeds of the license plate sale. It should be inscribed, "Here lies Carl Lindstrom, who so loved his license plates that he gave his life for them."

If he would only have sold a few hundred, he might not have starved to death. That is just what happened back in the early 70's.

No. 2764, the 24″ White Horse, $6,500-$7,500

28

DEALING FOR THE RAREST METTLACH STEIN IN THE WORLD ON THE NEW YORK CITY FREEWAY

In 1973, when I was known as Mr. Mettlach, the stein king of the U.S., I received a letter from a New York city man offering me the rarest Mettlach stein in the world, the six-liter White Horse, at a very reasonable price. He also had for sale cheaply the five-liter Socrates.

We made arrangements to go East and buy these two krugs (large trophy steins). Fran and I sat back comfortably, while our foster son, Ed, did the driving. I was very leary of taking several thousand in cash into New York city, so I made plans to meet the seller on the New York city freeway in Connecticut. However, in spite of my precautions, I began to feel that our last moment on earth might be approaching, as we got closer to the meeting place. Big city hustlers have been known to do away with people for a lot less than the $3,000 I was expecting to pay for the steins.

As we drove up to the place where we were to meet on the turnpike, I told Ed to back into the parking spot and point our car in the direction of traffic. I wanted to be sure that if anything looked suspicious, Ed could pull straight out into heavy traffic and get lost.

After a long wait, we spotted our man on the other side of the highway. He parked and came across, carrying his box containing the steins. As he showed them to us, he said that he had been a bartender at the Waldorf-Astoria, and while there had made friends with an old German couple who used to come in for a beer and a chat two or three times a week. When both got older and could no longer make the trip downtown, they came into the bar one day with the two big steins, and gave them to him for his kindness.

I paid the old bartender a fair price for the rare six-liter White Horse, which sold at that time for $4,500, and gave him his asking price for the Socrates.

The six-liter White Horse was my first 26″ rare Mettlach stein, and I was destined to own two more of them. Records of the Stein Club International, of which I am a member, shows no one else has ever owned over two six-liter White Horse steins.

After concluding our deal, Ed pulled into the heavy flow of New York-bound traffic, and then veered east.

I felt even more elated after we stopped in Ohio and bought another five-liter Mettlach Symphonia stein, and a half-liter rare White Horse to take back, along with a car full of rare, early American antique quilts and dated coverlets at pre-arranged stops. It used to be fun going antiquing before there were so many of us.

29

SNOOKERING FLINTFACE
OUT OF A PAIR
OF RARE DRY SINKS

It was 1974, the year that my partner and I located seven high-backed dry sinks all within six weeks--a record we would never again equal. In fact, we were never to see one more high-backed dry sink for sale again!

Our fourth and fifth dry sinks were located near Lena, Illinois, where Nate and I had gone to a sale, he in his old maroon pick-up truck, and I with my panel truck, to see if a dry sink advertised on the sale bill was indeed a high-back with drawers above, as the sale bill said.

When we got to the auction we saw a fine old dry sink standing there with some other common furniture, but around the dry sink were three hard-nosed and high-bidding primitive furniture dealers. One was "Flintface" Harriet Frazer, the roughest of all the area dealers to bid against.

While waiting for the sale to begin, Nate over-heard a woman standing next to him ask Harriet if she would be interested in another dry sink, which she had at her farm. She told Harriet it was just like the one at the auction, and added that she had some nice old bottles to sell, too. They agreed that Harriet would come directly from the sale, as soon as the dry sink there was sold, to look at the one on the farm.

It was Nate's lucky day to overhear such a con-versation. He went right over to the lady who had spoken, and told her he collected bottles. He said he overheard that she had some, not mentioning the dry

A low-backed pine dry sink from Pennsylvania with tongue-and-groove con-struction, circa 1820, $995. Author's Collection.

sink. He was told he could come and see them whenever he wanted, as she did not plan to stay at the sale
to see the dry sink sold.

I warned Nate to get moving, or Flintface would
beat him to the farm. I myself left for what I hoped
was a better sale in Freeport.

Nate got in his truck, arriving at the farm even
before the owner did. When she drove in, Nate asked
if she happened to have any dry sinks for sale. She
told him that she did have one, and that it was upstairs
in the barn loft.

Nate took the loft steps two at a time, and saw to
his amazement not one, but two, high-backed Pennsylvania dry sinks with original red paint, and hardly
showing any use. Nate developed strength he did not
know he had as he hauled the two sinks down the
steep ladder by himself. He knew time was of the
essence. He knew the high-backed sink at the auction
was now sold, and Flintface would be driving up at
any moment.

Nate made a fast $75-each deal for the fine old
$600-each-retail sinks. The owner would have sold
much more cheaply, but Nate knew he had to close
the deal in a hurry.

As he was paying, the owner of the sinks asked
him, "Don't you want to take a look at the bottles? You
said that is what you wanted to buy. I've got some good
ones."

Helpless to escape, Nate took a fast look at the bottles along the barn wall, and saw they were all
common.

"You can sell those to Harriet Frazer when she
comes," Nate said, "I know that's the kind she buys."

And with that, Nate drove out of the circular farm

drive with the two dry sinks in his truck just as Flint-face and her helper were driving in.

Our seventh high-backed dry sink was found up north of Freeport, where the auctioneer had advertised it as "a tall pine piece with drawers for screws." We bought it, grease and all, for $30.

The dry sink at the Lena sale, we found out, brought $475, and Harriet bought it. I have often wondered what her reaction was when she found that Nate had bought the other two dry sinks offered her for $75 apiece.

Harriet Frazer did not speak to Nate Ross or me for seven years afterward because of this deal, which she guessed I master-minded, and today she is only saying a brief hello.

30

THE "METAL" LAMP
THAT TURNED OUT TO BE THE
FABULOUS TIFFANY LABURNUM

During 1981 an event occurred in the Tiffany lamp world that is still being discussed wherever Tiffany dealers and collectors congregate. On a hot July Wednesday, a sale was conducted in Rockford, Illinois, by the Roy Stenzel Auction Service. That service is still being cussed by all the big and little antique dealers who were cheated out of attending this sale by an ad in the local paper that made no mention of the great signed Tiffany Laburnum floral table lamp to be sold, a lamp that is shown in Dr. Egon Neustadt's Tiffany book as one of the greatest Tiffany masterpieces. How those who made up the much-talked-about sale bill could have fallen into such a grievous error as to call a 1,000-pane scalloped-rim glass lamp a "metal lamp" was a big mystery to all the lamp and art glass dealers within a 75-mile radius who constantly watch the newspapers for just such a possible bargain.

Only later did I hear what happened in Rockford on that unbelievable day. The auction crew arrived at the place of the sale at the usual time, 5 a.m., and began moving the contents of the house outdoors to be ready for the 11 a.m. starting time. This auction was no different from any of the other 3,000 or more sales that Roy Stenzel and Bert Nichols had cried, or so they supposed.

By 7 a.m., most of the upstairs furniture, with a smattering of antiques, was already outside. About this time a Rockford antique dealer and lamp collector, Al Lenox, drove up early as per usual at a Stenzel sale to look the old glass and lamps over to see if he could find a sleeper anywhere. Art glass and signed lamps were the meat of this dealer, an old friend of mine whom I had helped locate some very rare signed Pairpoint scenics and puffies.

One of the auction crew, recognizing Lenox, asked him to go down into the cellar and take a look at a lamp down there to see if it was signed. Lenox walked down the flight of steps to look at the "metal" lamp he had seen advertised. What he saw almost dropped him. Instead of the cheap, old metal lamp he had expected, he saw standing next to the coal bin and covered with a half century of coal dust, one of the most beautiful Tiffany lamp masterpieces in the world. It was the 28″ by 21″ small version of the Laburnum with 1,000 or more floral panes of favrile glass.

The elderly lady owner had bought this lamp at a local garage sale for $1 some years before, she had told the auctioneer, and had let it sit in her basement ever since. She was the one who had made out the sale bill, I was told later by the sale clerk. She did not want strangers going through her house.

It was she who had called the great 1,000-panel flowering Laburnum a "metal lamp," and what happened afterward was her own fault for not allowing the auction crew in the house to list her sale items. Her mistake was to cost her a small fortune.

As Lenox came up out of the basement, he was met by Stenzel, who asked him if he liked the lamp and if it was signed anywhere. Lenox said he hadn't noticed. Actually, he had found it was signed "L. C. Tiffany Studios, NYC." and was also numbered.

This discovery caused Lenox, as he told me later, to go to his bank immediately and borrow $50,000 to make sure that no one was going to buy that lamp away from him for under $50,000 that day. Cash is what Stenzel demands at all his auctions, because he has been burned with two bad out-of-state checks, and doesn't mean to get burned again.

At this time, a furniture dealer who knew just enough about Tiffany lamps to be a dangerous bidder, arrived on the scene. He was Nick Wilde, from Beloit, Wisconsin. As Nick told me a few days later, he got there around 9:30 a.m., intending to see if there was any furniture he could use in his Beloit auction house.

Wilde took one look at the big beautiful flowering Tiffany lamp now standing in the center of a table in the back yard, and knew he would need a lot of help to buy it if A. Lenox should happen to show up, as he usually had at antique sales during the previous ten years. Wilde drove right out to Rock City Antiques to see Gordy, the owner and his sometimes-partner, and discuss what they could do to buy the finest Tiffany lamp that had ever surfaced in recent memory in the Midwest. The auction would start in just an hour, so time was of the essence to dig up all the cash possible and buy the lamp away from Lenox.

All the cash that Gordy could come up with was $13,000, which Nick distributed in several wads in various pockets.

The sale began as Bert Nichols asked for a $1,000 starting bid. The elderly lady owner had told the auctioneers that she would not take less than $600 for the lamp. "If it doesn't bring that," she told Stenzel, "it will go back in my house."

What a gross understatement of lamp price that was! The bidding between Wilde as Gordy's front man and Lenox got started with a big bang, as both bidders laid into each other with $100 raises that sometimes turned into $500 and even $1,000 jumps up to $5,500.

This phenomenal bidding caused Nichols to take off his big cowboy hat and look around perplexed, as if asking himself, could those bids he had heard be for real? The first few spirited seconds of bidding had already, at 20% commission, put $1,000 into the sale commission kitty.

During the pause, Nick asked Mary Stenzel if he could come inside the closed-off area to see if the lamp was signed Tiffany. Mary became annoyed at this hold-up in the sale and replied, "What's the difference if it's signed or not signed? All you're doing, Nick, is holding up the sale."

But Nick was allowed to take off the lamp top to check for the signature around the rim and on the base, and then the greatest bidding match in Rockford-area recent history resumed.

Soon the bidding was up to $13,000, with Nick the

The Laburnum, $50,000-$55,000 today.

very nervous $13,000 bidder. Without hesitation, Lenox bid $13,500. Then all of a sudden it was all over on the Rockford lamp battle front. Nick and Gordy were out of cash. The new owner was an elated Al Lenox. He emptied his pockets of several rolls big enough to choke a cow, and paid off in $100 bills. It was probably more money than the auction crew had ever seen at once before.

I heard all about the lamp battle the next morning through a friend who had been present. He knew fine lamps, but as a retired school teacher, he could only look. From his description, I identified the lamp as the small size Laburnum Tiffany masterpiece.

At once I called a lamp expert in Flint, Michigan, to inform him of what had just happened at a little-advertised sale in Rockford. He told me to call Lenox with a $50,000 cash offer for the lamp. I would get a 10% finder's fee, or $5,000, if the deal went through and the lamp was perfect.

When I called Lenox and stated my offer, he immediately said no, adding that the lamp was worth a lot more. That is the end of that, I told myself. Apparently Al knew the real worth of the best lamp ever to surface at a small Midwest auction.

Not a week later I noted that another Laburnum was to be sold at Sotheby's big eastern auction gallery, and was pictured in that month's **Antiques** magazine. I wrote the gallery for the results of that Laburnum's sale. The reply informed me that $85,00 had been the price.

After I got the report back from Sotheby's, I started to steam at the thought of having lost a potential $50,000 + profit. I was not the only one. Not long after, I bumped into a Rockford dealer named Betty Jamison who has a great penchant for anything Tiffany. She describes herself as a bad-tempered Italian who married a dumb Swede. When I asked her if she had heard about the lamp deal, she emitted as violent a stream of four-letter words as I had ever heard a man use, let alone a lady. For a solid hour, as a sale was going on, she kept swearing at Stenzel and his crew. The dummies should have known how valuable the lamp was after it was lifted up out of the basement, and held it back for a future sale where it could be properly advertised, she said.

"My Dad and I had $50,000 to bid, and we would have given Lenox a run for his money. They won't even believe me when I tell them how much the lamp was really worth," she moaned. "It would have sold for close to $100,000, and this is what I've told them whenever I go out to a sale. Now those auctioneers are mad at me for telling them the truth and how they are out a $16,000 commission."

After this fussing and cussing had subsided, I told Betty about the $85,000 Laburnum auction report along with the picture I had of the lamp. We hatched a good way of getting at the Stenzels for cheating us out of the once-in-a-lifetime chance to own a great Tiffany lamp and not just an ordinary geometric Tiffany. I told Betty I'd mail her the auction report and she could take it to the next Stenzel sale.

The next Stenzel auction saw Betty there early, carrying the Sotheby's report and the color picture. At the appropriate time before the sale, Doris went up to Bert Nichols and let him see and read the lamp report. She said he turned red, and his big cowboy hat nearly melted over his ears. Then Roy Stenzel read it, and the veins on his neck got so red and enlarged that his shirt collar nearly choked him. Then Mary Stenzel read it, and charged into the house where she stayed for the rest of the sale.

Although it has been two years since the Laburnam was sold, I am only slowly getting over this lamp deal myself. At the time, I was furious that I didn't own the great Tiffany lamp instead of Al Lenox. This is what the love of money will do to you. It will make you hate your best friends out of plain old jealousy.

As a warning to those who might want, like Lenox, to hold on to their finds for larger profits later, Lenox still owns his lamp, and may for a long time to come. All lamps have taken a precipitous drop in prices due to the state of the economy.

"I cannot sell them," Lenox told me recently over the phone. "They are down 30 to 60% at the big Eastern gallery sales."

31

MY STRANGE
INTRODUCTION
TO THE F.B.I.

In 1973 the biggest Mettlach stein robbery that had ever occurred up until that time took place at Dr. Nord Engel's house in Elgin. I had gotten to know Nord and Eliza Engel quite well because I had sold them many of the biggies--three to seven-liter steins that they preferred over the half and one-liter sizes. Trade journals carried all the details of the robbery and announcement of a $40,000 reward for the arrest and conviction of the thieves.

To avoid such a theft, Dr. Engel had made it a practice to make periodic checks of his home during the day from the nearby General Mills testing lab where he worked. But in between checks, the well-organized team of professional thieves, who had parked their truck near the Engel home, carried out all the big 18″ to 28″ tall steins, and carefully placed them in the compartments of liquor packing boxes (one of which they left behind.) They made a clean get-away in less than 30 minutes, and when Engel drove back for his check, his stein collection and several other great Mettlach rarities were gone.

The news of the stein burglary spread like wildfire throughout the Mettlach world. Dr. Engel had every stein indelibly marked with a number, so the word was passed from dealer to dealer and to all the 1,100 Stein Club International members to be on the alert for these numbers and call the police in Elgin and the F.B.I. if any attempt was made to sell such a numbered stein.

The next evening, after I heard about the big heist, I was busy down at my barn unloading oak furniture with my two boys when an old black car pulled in my yard and parked next to where we were unloading. An average-dressed man walked up to me carrying a brief case. When I spotted it, I figured the guy was selling something, so I told him right now, "Whatever you're selling, I don't want any, so goodby. We're busy here."

When the guy didn't move, but instead reached in his pocket and flipped open an identification wallet, I learned why he didn't move. This was an F.B.I. agent! I melted down from a big iceberg into a small puddle. Seeing those credentials scared the heck out of me.

The stranger told me he was an agent for the Rockford F.B.I. office, and was sent down to talk to me about Dr. Engel's steins being stolen. The more he talked, the more I kept staring at his worn-out old suit and even sadder-looking old car. All the while my mental image of what F.B.I. agents should look like was being deflated. I guess I had watched too many

TV shows.

The agent asked me to show him what steins I had on hand. I took him to the house, and he carefully inspected all the steins and made notes. After an hour of this, he said goodby, adding we'd be in touch, and drove away in the old car. I still had my doubts he was a real agent, but when I called the Rockford office, they confirmed it.

Some years after the theft of the steins that the Engels loved so dearly, Fran and I were travelling to the Cleveland Stein Club convention with them, and I brought up the robbery. Dr. Engel told me that shortly after his steins with the unremovable numbers on their bases were stolen, the half-liter cameo steeple stein that I had sold him in 1970 turned up in St. Louis. A dealer, seeing the tell-tale number, turned it over to the F.B.I., which in turn gave it back to Dr. Engel. It was the only half-liter he owned. All the rest were big steins.

To this day, Dr. Engel has not heard anything more about his stolen collection. He told me there was no way on God's green earth that the thieves could rub out the numbers. I answered him, "Dr. Engel, for money, anything is possible."

For years afterward, I kept the F.B.I. agent's visit in mind as I advertised in all the national papers and magazines to help Engel replace the big steins that had been stolen. This was practically accomplished when a big national price rise in 1977 and 78 virtually ended the chance for any collector to amass such a collection again.

No. 2201, the 19″ etched Socrates, $2,300.

32

THE FLOATING
JEWELRY STORE
CON GAME

In 1980, things were going along fine in the mail-order antique business, and because I was making lick after lick, I thought I could do no wrong. Remembering that I'd bought a few good things from an old man named Chris Holland, I decided to pay him a visit at his farm north of town. He was a Chicago retiree and tough to take on. He had formerly owned a block-long factory, and now owned several farms. I had made only a minimal profit on items I had bought from him, but I was always hoping he'd go to the bank and bring back the cigar box full of gold coins he told me was cached there, or the big five-karat diamond ring his first wife had worn until she died.

On this visit, Chris told me he had something in his garage that I might be interested in. He came back carrying a box of antique wood carvings of the whole

Andy Gump family. All were beautifully carved and stood on a 2″-high block. There was Andy and Junior and the Gump maid. He said a dentist in Chicago had done the carving. He asked me $1,000 for the finely carved figures, and I reeled back, saying, "Are you nuts?"

After several more trips out there, I made a deal to give him the thousand only if a dealer I knew would buy the figures. The dealer bought the carvings at a good profit to me, and the next time I visited the O'Hare Antique Show, I saw the five Gump figures in a top show dealer's booth priced at $8,900.

This made me even more hungry to buy the big diamond that Chris continually kept describing as big as a headlight. He said it had been purchased years before at the famous Peacock's Jewelry Store in downtown Chicago. In the early days if you bought it at Peacocks, you'd be buying the best.

Later that year I stopped to see Chris and asked again about the Peacock diamond. This was my day, because he had brought it home and had it hidden away. When he brought it out, he carried as well a lovely, large cameo and a few more pieces of his first wife's jewelry that I quickly added up as worth $1,000. Then Chris told me to hold onto my hat, I'd really see something, and he opened the ring box, where I saw what looked to be a diamond, sparkling truly as big as a headlight. It was the biggest diamond I had ever seen, and along its Tiffany platinum filigree mounting were eight smaller diamonds on each side. The setting was gorgeous. After my heart slowed down its violent thumping, I asked Chris how much.

He snarled out, "twelve thousand dollars, or it goes back down to the bank. I'll let you have her other pieces of jewelry to sweeten the pot."

With Chris, I'd found you better buy while he was in the mood. The next time around he would have gotten his price from some other person and would taunt you with it.

Chris told me he used to work for a Chicago jeweler years before, and the diamond looked like over five karats to him. I thought to myself, if his first wife was as well off as he told me, and as the photo albums he had shown me indicated, and if the diamond was purchased at Peacock's, which the case indicated, then I couldn't miss as to its being a perfect diamond. This is why it never once occurred to me that the diamond could be glass or a zircon, or full of black carbon spots rendering it worthless. It could be worth a lot of money in profit to me, I figured.

I told Holland to hold the diamond, and I'd go to the bank and get the money.

"Don't bring me any checks, or I'll warn you, the diamond is going back to the bank," he said.

I got in my car, and at high speed took off to see about a 90-day loan. I envisioned a week at Las Vegas, with a trip to the Riviera where I'd play roulette, after which I'd buy a chalet in the Alps and watch skiers through the windows while drinking hot toddies. The Peacock diamond might fall into the A grade in quality, like diamonds I had seen at Cherryvale Mall near Rockford, where one karat was priced at $95,000! This meant I might be buying five times $95,000, or a $475,000 five karat diamond for $12,000!

Back at Holland's I knocked on the front door, thinking I would now be even for all the antiques he had sold me for too-high prices. No answer. I began to think the greedy old man had gone to Sterling to have the diamond appraised. I was about to go away, when I heard a noise out by the barn. It was Chris moving a ladder, getting ready to paint his barn at 82 years of age.

Chris asked me if I had the $12,000 cash, and I showed him a big manila envelope crammed with money.

"I'll go get the ring," Chris said. He went to the house, and he went into another room. When he came back, he snapped open the Peacock box, and I nearly keeled over as once more I saw the diamond, big and sparkling in its magnificent platinum mounting.

This has to be worth a half-million dollars, because these people owned a block-long factory, I thought. I handed Holland the $12,000 worth of $100 bills with hands that were shaking so bad that the last few thousand were counted out by Chris. It was my biggest purchase in 50 years of being a wheeler-dealer. Chris threw in a big diamond stick pin to boot, and I left thinking I had just made the most profitable deal in all the thousands of my antique career. I kept feeling to see if the ring was secure in my pocket as I high-tailed it back to Viller's Jewelry Store in Dixon to hear their appraisal price.

Sam looked at it hard with his loupe and told me it was a nice stone, which seemed to need cleaning, and after he did that he could get to work on an appraisal. I told Sam I'd just as soon take it home to surprise my wife with first, and then I'd bring it back.

When I showed the diamond to Fran, she damned near had a snit fit to hear I'd paid $12,000 cash for it.

"You'd better get it looked at," she said. "I don't trust that greedy Holland as far as I can throw an elephant by the tail. I've seen the shady deals he's given you. Besides, it doesn't look like five karats, and it doesn't even look like a real diamond.''

That was enough to make me throw my car into high speed and head for Steiner's Jewelry Store in the Sterling Mall for a quick appraisal. When I showed the ring to the registered gemologist, he said the appraisal would take three days.

The next three days were hell for me, thinking I had made a big mistake buying the crafty Chicagoan's diamond. Hadn't he told me he used to work in a jewelry store? This was no pigeon, I thought, instead I might be the pigeon.

No, this could not be, I'd tell myself. Sam Villers looked at the ring and called the diamond a good stone.

On the third day, I was at Steiner's when the doors opened. I paid $50 for the appraisal and the return of my diamond, and quickly tore open the envelope. There I read that the diamond was an S-1 and J grade stone. This meant it was free of carbon spots and the brilliance was good. The J color grade was the affordable grade that most jewelers sell. It was not a five karat stone as Chris had said, but a 3.2 karat diamond, and mine-cut (old cut). The appraisal was $18,000. I was not ecstatic over this, but relieved that the ring, at least, wasn't a dud.

At least I would be able to sell it for a good profit, I thought, and now would be able to shut up Fran, who had been harping on me all day every day since the purchase for pulling this dumb stunt, when, she said, she could hardly buy herself a dress.

I showed Fran the appraisal. 'Who's going to give you $18,000?'' she asked.

I decided the best outlet for the ring was a jewelry store. I drove to Rockford and made the rounds of the leading jewelers. Not a single one was interested. Each said the stone was mine-cut, and this type of cut did not sell for them.

"The ladies like the cutting to cover the diamond and be flat on top," they said.

At last I went into Libbey's in the old downtown business district. The store reminded me of the heyday of downtown Rockford with its opulence. Old man Libbey himself got out his loupe to examine my diamond, and asked me now much I wanted for it. He would buy it if the price was right. Embarrassed to ask a high price after being insulted at three or four other jewelers', I asked Libbey if he'd give me $10,000.

Libbey said, "No, thanks, but I do know where you can sell it in Chicago, at the Friedberg Building. A friend of mine has a shop there. He'll pay you more than I can, because he has the customers for a stone your size and price. He'll take an hour or so to examine the diamond, as he'll have to take it out of its setting and put it in the washer before he can approve it for himself." Libbey handed me a piece of paper with a name on it.

Before heading out the next day for Chicago, I chanced to meet Villers, my Dixon jeweler, on the street. When I told him my destination, he said he had heard that many diamonds were expertly switched in the back rooms of the Friedberg Building. He said the Friedberg Building guys were so expert they could open all the prongs on my Tiffany mounting in less than four minutes, and put the ring back together with a cheap diamond filled with flaws. This was all the warning I needed.

I asked Sam if I could improve my selling chances by getting the diamond recut from mine-cut to brilliant new cut, and he answered that it would definitely improve my chances. He said he could send the ring to New York and have it back in six weeks with a new look, for $600.

I thought of this offer for awhile, and then one day I took my diamond ring off Fran's finger, where she was wearing it behind another tight ring, and took it to town to have it sent away.

In six weeks, Villers called to say the ring was back. When I walked up to the counter, Sam had the ring box out, and grinning broadly, snapped it open to reveal the ring shimmering in the light as if it were a huge piece of tinsel off a Christmas tree. I couldn't help staring at my own diamond as it glistened and caught the reflection of the overhead lights, casting a rainbow of color in every direction. Even Sol Viller put down his watch repair work and came over to look at the diamond. It now weighed 2.6 karats, Sam said, a loss of just over ½ karat.

"Who cares?" I said, "if it will please my wife." I pulled out six $100 bills with a dash of arrogance, thinking meanwhile to myself that I now had $12,650 invested in my sparkler.

I took the ring home and showed it to Fran. If she loved it before, it now turned her ape, and she ran under light after light in the house, making it into a 4th of July sparkler. If she fell in love with it anymore, I wouldn't be able to get it away to sell it, so I broke the bad news that the bank was not going to extend the loan, and it had to go. Reluctantly, I took the ring off her finger, and began an advertising blitz.

I had calls all the way up to my neck from my

newspaper ads. All wanted to know the price at once, and when I'd say, $12,650," they'd either hang up, or say, "You must be nuts, wasting my long distance call money with your crazy prices." It didn't take long for me to find out that you just couldn't sell a diamond like that without appraisal from a well-known jeweler.

I thought I'd better get the ring re-appraised, now that it had been recut, so I took it back to Villers. It didn't take them three days, either. They did it in about a minute at no charge. When I opened the envelope, I received a shock. Instead of the $18,000 of the year previous, it was now appraised at $25,000!

I am going to unload this ring on someone now, I told myself, or throw it in the drink.

I put an ad in the Rockford paper reading, "For sale, brilliant cut, 2.6 K diamond ring in a platinum open filigree setting with 16 small diamonds, $10,000.'.

I waited a week for a reaction. Right at the end of the ad's run, I received a call from a lady who told me she lived on Ritzy Road in Rockford, and would be driving down with her fiance' to eat in a Grand Detour restaurant, and would like to stop and see the ring. We agreed on a time, and not a minute late, a knock on my door signalled the beginning of one of my most bizarre experiences.

I admitted a svelte, 50-ish woman with hair piled high in a bun, wearing a mink jacket and flashing several diamonds. Her swarthy boyfriend was also well-dressed. They said they were planning an October wedding, and he was looking for a good diamond to seal the nuptials. The lady raised her hand to show off what she had on her fingers, given her by her first husband who had taken off the year before and left her, she said.

She told me she loved my ring, as she waved it first this way and then that on her finger. After a conference between the two of them, her lover told me, "I'll be paying for it, so before I do, I'd like you to bring the ring to our jeweler's in Rockford for them to look at it. Ten thousand dollars is a lot of money for a ring we know nothing about."

The time and place I'd meet the lady was set and she handed me her card showing her address along Millionaire's Row. At 10 a.m. the next day I arrived there with my diamond locked up in my car dash. I didn't want to risk getting my head bashed in for it by flashing it around in a stranger's house. As I got out, I wondered why anyone living in a $200,000 stone house would lower herself to read classified sale ads. When I recognized both a Mercedes and a Jaguar sports car in her garage, I was sure she didn't have any business reading the classifieds. Yet it looked like I would have no sweat in getting my $10,000 if her jeweler agreed the diamond was perfect.

When I knocked and was admitted to the house, I saw such opulence as I thought possible only in the 30's movies. Everything in the house looked like old money. After I was shown her ex-husband's stein collection, I said we had better get going to the jeweler's. I had asked her on the phone where the jewelry store was, and she had told me it was behind Rock River Towers, a respectable building housing a score of business places. I'd looked hard for the jewelry firm as I'd driven by on my way to her house, but had seen nothing of it behind the Towers in the mini-mall of stores.

Yet as I followed her Mercedes to the Towers building, I had nothing but positive vibes that I'd soon be back home with her $10,000 cashier's check in my hands, and at last be out from under the curse of the Peacock diamond.

Instead of walking back to the row of mall stores, my customer motioned me to the building's back entrance. I began looking, without luck, for a big jewelry store on the parking lot level, but my buyer quickly walked to the elevators and pushed floor 5. I wondered what the hell was going on as the elevator shot us up. What kind of jewelry store could make good on the fifth floor? As I followed the svelte lady, I began to feel that something was wrong, but I could not convince myself to run for it, because I was so anxious to sell my high-priced mistake. I would take my $2,600 loss like a good antique dealer should, and never fool around with diamonds again.

I was ushered into a small room with one small, five-foot glass showcase displaying some costume jewelry and a watch or two. I heard Mrs. X ask a big guy in back of the counter for the owner. He answered that his dad was out to lunch and wouldn't be back for an hour or more. When Mrs. X mentioned who she was and that she had an appointment, he turned and hollered something into a back room.

Out came the owner and supposed appraiser and shook hands with my buyer. He asked to see the ring I was holding on to tightly by now in my coat pocket. He said he'd have to take it to his back room and wash it. I now felt I was in some sort of clip joint, but with Mrs. X standing there with her big diamonds, I weighed how she looked against the looks of the place, and handed my ring over for cleaning. Was my diamond going to be removed and replaced with an inferior stone as I had heard would happen in the

Friedberg Building?

This thought spun in my head as I stood for ten or 15 minutes with my $10,000 stone out of sight. For the first time, I noticed a jeweler's scope standing on a small table nearby. I'd never seen anything like that standing out in front of a showcase in any of the jewelry stores I'd been in.

Finally the appraiser came out of his back room with a smile and my diamond. He ushered us over to the scope and invited Mrs. X to sit at his left and me at his right while he looked at the diamond for any imperfection. Not one second had passed before he said, "There's a tadpole (a slang term for a carbon spot in the stone, making it imperfect.) I see two more tadpoles."

Here he asked an uneasy Mrs. X to look at the tadpoles through his scope, and as she did, he asked her, "Do you see them?"

Her face crimson with embarrassment, she answered, "yes."

I now knew the clip was on. When the crooked jeweler asked me to look at the tadpoles, I yelled at him, "You dirty crook, hand over my ring or I'll bust you and your place up!"

He shakily raised his hand with the ring held in it, and as he did, I grabbed it so fast from his outstretched fingers that I nearly took them off, all the time calling both Mrs. X, who had turned even more crimson, and him every dirty, foul-mouthed name I had in my dirty-word vocabulary learned in the streets. All in one move, I ran out of the so-called jewelry store, cursing them loudly all the way to the elevator, and trying to get out of there before the cops would arrive. I knew the crooked jeweler would call them after he had gotten over the initial shock of nearly having his hand wrenched off and being cussed at so hard.

As I tore out of Rockford, I began to think hard about what I had been told about the Chicago diamond buyers who could remove a stone while pretending to wash it. The more I thought about it, the more speed I got on my car, until I went down Cement Plant Hill north of Dixon and saw my speedometer standing at 105 miles an hour.

I immediately called Sam Villers at his home. He said I could bring the ring right out and he would look at it. "If they've switched your diamond, I'll personally go up there and ring their necks," he said.

Sam told me he didn't have a loupe for examining stones at his home, but didn't need one. He said he had always loved big diamonds, and when he had first seen mine, he had memorized what it looked like. After one look, he assured me, "This is your original diamond, Dan, and it is a beauty."

I then went into another advertising blitz in all the surrounding towns, but without a nibble. My wife suggested I wear the diamond in my nose.

Almost four months had gone by since the Mrs. X altercation. I couldn't help thinking of all the suckers Mrs. X and her boy friends had enticed into their disreputable "jewelry store," conning old people out off their diamonds and emeralds, saying they were crawling with tadpoles, and suggesting, "Here, take a look yourself." I feel the jeweler's scope was rigged with carbon spots in the lens.

In desperation one day, I dialed the largest jewelry store in Freeport, Bradley's. Old man Bradley himself answered, and I told him I'd like to sell my mother's diamond ring, which I described as an almost three

karat stone, brilliant cut with platinum filigree mounting and set with 16 more small diamonds. I lowered
my price to $7,500, a loss of $6,000 cash.

For the first time, I was talking to someone who
sounded like he bought diamonds. We made an appointment for the next day.

Once more I had to make Fran take the gorgeous
ring off her finger. She had become progressively
fonder of it, as it left a trail of sparkles that made other
women envious.

As I entered Bradley's, I saw on the door that they
had been founded 100 years before, and that reassured
me that they would not pull a Mrs. X deal. Mr. Bradley
took me on a tour of his beautiful old store while his
son did an appraisal. The son, a new graduate of San
Francisco's School of Gemology, agreed with the
previous rating of the stone as S-1 brilliant, which he
said was very good, and graded the color J, which is
average. He said the stone was 2.62 karats, and a very
beautiful cutting.

It was the moment of truth, whether Bradley
would buy it or not. His bid was a low $6,000.

I asked for my ring back, saying I wasn't in the
mood to play games. Bradley quickly offered $6,500,
and that was, he said, his very best price. I told him
I'd have to call my wife, as she loved the ring, and
didn't want me to sell it in the first place. Mr. Bradley
pointed to his inside phone, where I stood with the
reciever to my ear and pretended to talk to Fran. I kept
hollering back to Bradley, "She won't sell for $6,500,
Mr. Bradley, she said it will take $7,000." That was
down $500 from my asking price.

I hung up the phone to see if these tactics had
worked, and they did. The thought of such a big,

sparkling diamond going out of the store made Bradley say, "Let me see that diamond again."

After a moment of standing behind the jewelry counter, he said, "I'll give you your $7,000, because with the Christmas season coming, I may be able to sell it. First, my son will have to remove this old-fashioned mounting, and then we'll send it to San Francisco for grading and appraisal. It will then be put into a modern gold mounting by my son, and displayed at Christmas and then for Mother's Day if not sold. Those are our two best diamond-selling holidays." With that he wrote me a $7,000 check.

There hasn't been another such foolish buy committed by me in the $12,000 bracket. It is the $100, $500, and $1,000 bad antique buys that are threatening to sink my antique ship nowadays.

33

THE SALE THAT
SOLVED THE MYSTERY OF
THE BOARDED UP MANSION

One day in 1965, I was reading one of the several papers I subscribed to in order to spot juicy antique sales, when I read that the contents of an ante-bellum home in Princeton, Illinois, not 28 miles away, was to be sold at auction. As I read the sale bill, I saw that the sale was "loaded," which means everything was a highly collectible antique. I had been driving by this house on business every week since 1950, and every time, I would look back on it as it stood all alone with its unpainted-for-decades siding and boarded-up windows. It was as spooky a looking place sitting on a bit of a hill that a writer of ghost stories could dream up.

Now a two-day sale was to be held to close out the estate on a Saturday at the fairgrounds and the next day on the premises. That Saturday saw Fran and me, two hours ahead of the sale, turn in at the fair-grounds where the house's contents were spread out inside the largest building. It was an unbelievable sight even for a jaded old dealer like myself who was beginning to think that nothing I looked at in antiques anymore could give me a thrill. I changed my mind here, because every place I looked, there was something that would make me gasp as I'd point it out to my wife to make sure she didn't miss anything, which she isn't apt to do anyway.

There were a pair of Gay Nineties high-wheel wooden bicycles with thick rope for tires. On a table was a large selection of beautiful Burmese, Agata, pink satin, and even signed Tiffany, Steuben, and more pattern and cut glass than I had ever seen in one place.

There was another table with an early 1900's crystal set, and large and small dovetailed oak boxes containing rare radio-related objects. I determined right-off to buy this early radio collection.

I had heard rumors among dealers that the old house had been equipped in 1900 by the owner with its own electrical plant, with a generator in the basement weighing a couple of tons.

Something tragic, I heard, had happened in the house back in 1920 that had caused the owner to board it up as quickly as possible, not taking even the pet cat, whose skeletal remains were found on the kitchen table when the house doors were opened for the sale.

The crowd went crazy price-wise. Nothing was sold cheap, as the two auctioneers formed separate rings and the sale heated up. I kept looking over at first one auctioneer and then the other, running back and forth so I could bid on the things I wanted. When it was the turn of the early radio collectibles, I was standing there ready and waiting to bid. I bought them, and at once had Fran carry them out to our car with the few other things that I had been able to buy.

As we drove back home, I remarked to Fran that the next day would be clean-up day at the spooky old house. She answered that it would be a lot of fun going through the movie-type haunted mansion.

At the sale the day before, Fran had approached the estate's lawyer, and asked him if there were any more old magazines at the house such as we had bought a smattering of. "Yes," the attorney replied, and continued to tell that the whole attic of the house was full. There were so many there that there had been no way they could bring them all to the fairgrounds.

"The house is full of old radio and car books and everything else he collected," the lawyer said.

When Fran told me this, I walked over to him and offered him $10 to let me look around in the house. He grabbed the $10 and said he would meet us with a key the next day.

We arrived early and went looking through the home's big rooms. In one back room, there were 24 big dry cell storage batteries, each the size of one of today's car batteries. They were sitting next to each other and still connected as in 1910. Below, in a creepy basement room, sat a huge General Electric four-by-eight foot generator.

Next, we climbed up the attic steps, and there, scattered all over the big attic floor, we saw piles of antique radio magazines, early wireless and electrical magazines, and hundreds of rare car showroom manuals for every car, it seemed, ever made. A ton of *Saturday Evening Posts, Ladies' Home Journals* back to 1888, *Delineators*, and an almost complete run of

The Boarded Up Mansion.

rare *Theatre* magazines, plus *Popular Mechanics*, were all strewn across the place as if a whirlwind had scattered them. I quickly estimated there was at least $10,000 worth of paper goods on the attic floor.

I was at this time a national paper goods dealer well-known through my weekly ads. It was relatively easy for me then, in the 60's, to find old magazines in long runs that I could sell for from $2 to $10 each. As the 1960's closed, no more good magazines ever came my way again. It was just like a vein of gold that had been mined for a decade running out.

I was now confronted with the decision of asking Bill Edgecomb, one of the auctioneers, to auction the attic's contents either from upstairs or from outside. I guessed correctly that the auctioneers had never seen the contents of the attic, and had relied on their men to haul everything out of the house. I didn't have to think twice here. I said to myself, if just one dealer outdoors sees all this money in paper goods lying around, it will take a lot of the profit out of it for me.

I decided to take one or two pieces of vague-looking paper goods down to Bill and ask him to sell the attic contents from the yard. Bill agreed to this, and so help me, Hannah, I bought everything up there for my starting bid of $1! I almost keeled over backwards as he sold it to my number.

I told Fran and a couple of my youngsters to start hauling out the loot. I cautioned Fran to be sure to load out first all the hundreds of fine car showroom brochures for Cadillacs, Pierce-Arrow, Hudsons, Buicks, etc., along with the radio magazines that were very much sought after even then.

The auctioneer then took us to the back of the house to the big double cellar door to sell the 1906 generator, a black, Frankenstein-looking object that was the largest generator I had ever seen. I decided to buy it right off, and then the two dozen dry cell batteries upstairs in hopes I could sell them to a museum in Crystal Lake.

Buying the generator proved to be harder than expected, due to lively bidding for the copper inside it, valuable as junk. Then after I had bought the generator and the batteries, I had to hire a big wrecker to load the generator and bring it home. We made four trips with our station wagon to the old mansion, each time filling our car to the top with fine old magazines that kept me busy for months selling to customers around the nation. It was, without a doubt, my most memorable paper goods buy.

All of the rare radio equipment was soon sold to the curator of a Crystal Lake, Illinois, wireless and radio museum. He and his wife drove straight to Dixon when I called and described what I had purchased. Not only did he buy all of the radio collectibles for a goodly sum, but he also bought the GE generator and dry cell batteries. He was a very happy man as he drove out of my yard with a rare early Marconi crystal set on his lap. Only he knew how much it was worth. I have often wondered, but it is best I never know. I would get sick at how low a price I sold it for.

34

THOSE AREN'T DISHES
I'M INSURING, SIR!
THOSE ARE METTLACH PLAQUES!

Back in 1974, I received a letter from an Army officer in Berlin advising me that he had a Mettlach plaque to sell. The letter came in response to a wanted-to-buy ad I had placed in the *Antique Trader*. Complimentary copies of that magazine were being sent to all the Army PX's in Germany, and I was beginning to hear from both officers and enlisted men. They would scour Germany to find all the Mettlach steins and plaques they could. Big German dealers would write as well, but mostly with inferior goods to sell. They knew where to dispose of the good stuff.

The Berlin officer wrote me that he had a #2187 horse and rider plaque to sell. He said that on the plaque was a knight in armor riding a prancing black horse with a crackled gold sunset in the background. On the bottom of the 16″ diameter plaque was the

House of Hapsburg shield.

I picked up my Mohr's Mettlach price guide to see what had been left out of this unusually fine description. I found "etched" was missing, and that $1,500 was missing! The officer asked me only $450 for the plaque.

What he didn't know was that he was about to sell me a single plaque from the pair of most desired of all Mettlach plaques, the German "Cities" Plaques. The mate to it was #2188, the Hohenzollern Plaque.

The agreement to buy this important plaque was concluded via cable phone after I called the officer's base outside Berlin. I was to airmail him $450 plus $25 for professional crating. I didn't want anything to happen to that plaque!

I knew I had bought a rare first half of the two best plaques every made at Mettlach. My Mettlach mentor for several years, Dr. Nord Engel, was very excited about the prospect of my selling it to him.

Everything went off smoothly with the deal, and soon my plaque arrived via air mail at the Dixon Post Office. When I went to pick it up, I was surprised to see that the wood slat box was much smaller than any crate I would have used. I only prayed that my plaque was safe inside. I had previously had terrible luck in buying and selling these heavy and fragile ceramics. Too many had been broken coming and going for me ever to want to chance shipping one again, with the exception of the very special Cities Plaques.

I could hardly wait to get home and get the crate open to see for myself this great plaque that could get an old Mettlach pro like Dr. Engel so excited that he called me every day to inquire if it had arrived yet.

With every push down on the crow bar, I kept fearing that the great German Cities Plaque that had lasted unbroken for so many years, would be lying in pieces as I had found so many others.

When I got the plaque unpacked, I held it up where the sun could hit the crackled gold background, and it shown just as a sunset does in winter on the magnificent work of German ceramic art. The blanketed black horse was prancing exactly as shown in Mohr's price guide. The tough-looking knight astride it was just as pictured, with one exception. Now I was seeing it in vivid color.

This had to be my most important buy from Germany to date. Dr. Engel, in the meantime, kept calling me and asking if I had received the plaque yet. I would always tell him "not yet." As anxious as this

One of the Mettlach "Cities" Plaques

great Mettlach man was to buy this single plaque, I could imagine how he would have acted had I had the pair to sell. He kept calling, and I just kept on admiring my great Cities Plaque, hoping against hope, that I'd get another letter or another call offering another plaque to match the one I had. I needed the Hohenzollern Plaque, #2188, with the knight facing the other way on his black charger. Wouldn't that look wonderful up on my office wall, both horses and riders facing each other as they were made to be, a pair?

Then one day as I sat at home after working all day answering mail, a call came in from a young man in Milwaukee. I could hardly believe what I was hearing, that this young man had inherited some Mettlach steins and a plaque. It had a crackled gold background, he told me, and a black horse and rider with a drawn sword facing right! I nearly keeled over right there as I stood talking with my mouth hanging open. I hardly paid any attention to what steins he told me he had to sell. I only remember saying, "Bring 'em down and I'll take em." The price we agreed upon for the plaque was the same as for the Berlin plaque, $450.

To be able to do all this record fast buying over the phone seemed strange to me. The steins and the plaque had to be hot for this young guy to quickly accept all the prices I fired at him. It was all clear profit, he probably figured. All this went through my mind as I decided I had to take a chance.

It was agreed to meet at the Dixon Ramada Inn, with my buyer to call me when he got there. I estimated it would be 10:30 before he could arrive, but at 9 a.m. he called, and I was there in a flash. In a short time he had his money, and I had all his Mettlach steins and the most important Mettlach acquisition

I was ever to make outside of the three six-liter White Horses. By the greatest stroke of good luck ever afforded a Mettlach dealer, I had safely in my hands, wrapped in soft tissue paper, the mate to my plaque at home, #2188, The Hohenzollern Plaque. The greatest pair of Mettlach plaques ever made were now matched, I thought, as a perfect pair, a Mettlach dealer's and collector's dream.

When I got the new plaque home, I looked at both, and from the front they did indeed appear to be a perfect pair. But when I looked at the backs, I knew right away they could never be sold as a perfectly matched pair. To my sorrow, I saw that the date on the plaque from Germany said 00, while the Milwaukee plaque said 02. This meant that one plaque was made in 1900 and the other in 1902.

Something strange must have happened to the mates of these plaques after they were sold out of some fine store at the turn of the century. One theory is that they were broken while being hung on a castle or house wall, since they are heavy and hard to handle. Or relatives may have split them up on the demise of the owner. The latter is my best answer to why single great Cities Plaques occasionally float around in the market place.

Dr. Nord Engel, in the meantime, between buying several five to seven-liter etched Mettlach steins from me at reasonable prices, kept harping on the single German Cities Plaque theme. When was I expecting it? This went on for about three and a half or four months, until one day it was time for me to buy another new car (which Nord and his wife kept telling me they bought for me every year with the profit I was making off steins I sold them.) I called Doc and told him something unbelievable had happened. I had both plaques of the pair. I let him think I had received them both from the Army officer in Germany.

"Are they ever beautiful, Doc. Sure, I'll sell them to you. When can I come over?"

Doc was working at his job of testing out food at the General Mills plant not over two or three miles from his home when I called. He took off work to meet me at his house to see and buy the greatest pair of plaques ever made at Mettlach.

"What do you think of them, Doc?" I asked. "Aren't they a beautiful pair?"

"They are not a pair."

The dreaded Nord made me swallow hard.

Another of the Mettlach "Cities" Plaques

"Does it hurt that one was made in 1900 and the other in 1902, Doc?" I asked, with a sinking feeling in the pit of my stomach.

"It sure does hurt, Dan, because they are no longer an exact pair, made by the same Mettlach artisan at the same time."

Once more Dr. Engel with his statement had shown me just how knowledgeable he was. Whenever one of anything is made several years apart from the other, there will be some differences. Dr. Engel was known in the Mettlach world as the No. 1 man in steins and plaque know-how. In fact, the grateful Mettlach factory had given him a 12-piece setting of Mettlach dishes, each with a different animal or bird on it, for his help as a consultant.

As this recollection went through my mind, I knew that Doc was going to cut me down badly on the price he would pay for the mis-matched plaques. But Doc and I always resolved our price differences quickly. Even if he did cut my asking price down, he was the kind of guy I needed to coddle with bargain prices, because someday I'd need his advice on how much to pay for a rare stein or plaque. He had taught me all I knew about steins, and was also my best customer for three to seven-liters. No one else I knew then or now would ever share his secrets.

Doc bought each plaque separately at 30% lower than matched pair prices. He paid $2,400, which gave me not too bad a profit for back in 1974, when you could still go to a grocery store and for $30 to $35 fill a shopping cart up to the tip-top.

I wish I could have afforded to keep the Cities Plaques, because the one thing I like most of all in the animal kingdom is the horse. I can still see the great black horses facing each other as they moved into battle on these plaques, with a knight in armor astride each. The Cities Plaques summed up for me what Mettlach artistry was all about. It was not the Cities Plaques I sold that day in Elgin, but my heart.

The best of anything in its field needs a run for the roses every once in a while. So do Mettlach Cities Plaques. Their chance came at Elyna, Ohio, last summer at the great Mettlach sale held there. Examples of my once-owned plaques set a new high price of $11,500 for the pair.

35

MY FIFTY YEARS
AS AN
ANTIQUE DEALER

In 1929, I started to kindergarten at South Central School in Dixon, Illinois, where Ronald Reagan had graduated just five years before. While in school there, I was being tutored daily in the coin and U.S. stamp business by Harry Webber, a Dixon stamp dealer, and in the antique trade by a dealer who ran the only shop in Dixon and a wide area. They helped me because I loved those things (as well as wanting to make money to buy candy.)

My father had gone into the antique business earlier, at the same time running a busy restaurant. At age nine, with his help, I purchased a large U.S. stamp collection with many rare stamps in it. I immediately started to sell my stamps up and down First Street to stamp collectors whom I got to know fast.

In 1931 stamp collecting was the No. 1 hobby in

the world. Many times during the Depression I would make over ten times what I had paid for stamps. There always seemed to be money to buy good stamps. This holds true also in today's economy. The money will always be there to buy top-of-the-line antiques or objets d'art.

From that day forward, I have always said that more money could be made in poor times than in good times, because a lot more good things come up that can be bought right. If you buy something right, there is always a good chance you will sell it right.

I paid Dad back his loan, and at ten years of age, I was on my way in the stamp business. My ad was always in Dixon papers to buy stamps for highest cash prices. With everyone in this area flat broke in the 30s, you can imagine the response to my ad. It was heart-warming to a wheeler-dealer kid.

Then I decided to cash in on my knowledge gained from two years' study in coins. I asked a few of the Dixon merchants if minded my looking through their cash registers once or twice a week for good coins. They agreed, and soon I was making my rounds checking cash registers for Indian head pennies, "V" nickels, and seated liberty quarters and halves. I had good luck with the Indian head pennies and V nickels, but none in the tougher-to-find varieties. So I decided to incorporate coins with stamps in my wanted-to-buy ads. It was hard going. I was not able to do as well with coins as with stamps, so I quit coins for then.

I went to work in the antique business in earnest. I would pull my wagon down to the smelter on the west end of town where old cars were dumped and cast iron laundry stoves were made out of their molten metal. I asked the foreman if I could go out in the foundry's junk yard and look for things I could use in my business. He asked me what my business was, and I told him "the junk business." If I had told him "antique business," he would have charged a scavenger's fee. People were even then thinking that if you were in the antique business, you were getting rich.

In the meantime, Dad had gone out of the antique business. He had a sale and ended up selling the few antiques he had on hand for less than half of what he paid for them, and with the auctioneer's commission to pay, he really went in the hole. Local people in those days would hardly give a dime for the best antique going. It was the few tourists whom we all depended upon.

They continued to let me look for saleable items in the junk yard, where I could take anything made of brass, copper, or nickel. I found mostly car horns, all twisted and ornate, and sometimes a foot-long brass pair. I would take off the hood ornaments from ready-to-be-scrapped classic cars such as Cadillacs, Packards, and Lincolns. I would unscrew the gear-shift knobs which were swirled like candy. I used to sell them for a dime. I'd rather take my profit in small bites than not at all. That was one of my mottos.

I would sometimes spot a 12-cylinder, cast aluminum motor on a Cadillac or other classic car. My good Jewish friend, Joe Steinberg, would drive right down with his wrecker and hoist the 400-pound engine up to his truck. At two cents per pound, I would pick up $8. My friends and I all ate one-cent candy and drank five-cent pop for a month from this monumental find.

I would sell other items found in the scrap yard to a lady whose antique shop on the east edge of town carried only the best. She was located on the busy highway that brought Chicago and other area tourists across the Midwest, so she always did well in her business. For years she bought Indian arrowheads from me, and also crockery with wording or unusual painting on it.

This dealer also bought all the old pattern and flint glass I could find. The colored flint glass was her favorite. If I ever found old copper pieces such as apple butter kettles, or old iron kettles, she was glad to get them, as they were among her best sellers.

She would always be stock-piling good glass and fine French Haviland dishes for the future, she told me. In a few years the antique mania hit the country, and anything that looked old found a ready market.

My antique career was interrupted by the War, but I took it up again as a sideline afterward. At this time I was a grain farmer and livestock dealer as well. I turned to antiques exclusively about 1955. At that time Tiffany went begging. Sample prices were: vase, 13½″ tall, tulip-shaped, green and yellow, signed, $22.50; gas light shade, signed, 6″ diameter, $10; nut bowl set with six dishes, signed, $24.50.

At this same time, I would occasionally get unsigned Tiffany-type lamps. Some would have hundreds of panels of beautiful, flowered leaded glass. The best price I could get for a lamp of this quality up until 1968 was $25, if perfect. This is hard to believe today, with $100,000 and $200,000 prices paid for Tiffany's Dragonfly and Spiderweb table lamps.

The last, rare, unsigned Tiffany-type table lamp I came across I sold for $25 in 1964. I did a lot of begging all over the area to sell this lamp. All the dealers said to me, "Nobody wants Tiffany-type leaded lamps. We simply break the leaded glass out of all we find, and sell the brass leading to the junk man." This convinced me that I should sell the best lamp of that type I had ever found. My wife had to spend all day shining up its brass crown and brass chain or it would have been no deal.

This lamp still hangs in a local antique-decor night club in the vicinity. It has over 750 panels of flowers on its shade, and with its gilt over bronze crown, it is much admired.

I should have done with the lamp what the lady antique dealer did with the French Haviland, put it aside for better days. They came in 1974. Lamps like that one jumped first to $500, and now to $5,000.

I continued in the stamp and coin business as a side-line to my antique business until 1960. What I had been taught by my stamp and coin teacher back in the early 30's had made me good money up until this time. Then in the early 60's both stamps and coins began a big price advance that has never been headed. I had to make a choice of either specializing in stamps and coins full-time to make it, or to deal in antiques. I chose to make my life antiques, and I haven't regretted even one single solitary day of it.

In my 50 years in the antique business there is hardly anything of quality, or otherwise, that I haven't bought or sold or seen sell. I use this experience to help me bid at sales. I will not stop bidding on anything that looks like it will make me even a small amount of money.

As detailed elsewhere, I have been a Mettlach stein specialist for over 25 years. In 1950 I sold a half-liter Mettlach character stein, #2018, a bulldog with pewter collar, for $35. Now this same bulldog character stein sells for over $1,100. Today an average

Musterschutz steins: Boar, $2,000-$2,200; Wilhelm II, $1,400-$1,500; Gentleman Rabbit, $1,300-$1,400; Stag, $2,000.

A Pairpoint Puffie, $3,500. From a photo furnished by Ed Malakoff, River Edge, New Jersey

half-liter etched Mettlach stein sells for $450, with some very fine three-liters bringing $4,000, and six-liters, $7,500.

I have sold some great Mettlach wall plaques in my day. Of all the plaques sold, my favorites are the toadstool plaques and the beautiful 18″ Snow White plaque. This plaque sells today in excess of $3,000. Mettlach steins and plaques are collected by a special breed of men and women who are the very best. Through dealing I became close to them, and I wouldn't exchange this camaraderie for all the money on earth.

As I led the Mettlach stein world for several years, I also led the Royal Doulton character jug and figurine world for one decade, 1966 to 1976. I made the market for all 2,900 different Royal Doulton figurines when there was none, and I led the nation in dealing in Royal Doulton character jugs for that period, making a monthly change in my buy and sell prices.

I started paying $10 each for 1¼″ character jugs, and today I pay over $100.

In the 1960's I bought and sold hundreds of fine old brass beds, both solid and brass-wrapped. I located beds by placing ads in all newspapers of nearby towns with over 10,000 population stating how much I would pay. My buy price was $25 each in 1968, and from then until 1972 I bought beds like mad. The top of my station wagon was always loaded with four or so headpieces, with the bases inside. I stored the beds in my 100-foot barn warehouse while I advertised them, and sent many as far away as Seattle and California by Allied Van Lines.

I have sold through national ads and shipped a very rare 1790 Hepplewhite American sideboard to a Nashville customer, a crate of 36 antique car horns made of brass to Seattle, an old copper bathtub encased in wood to California, and much, much more in this stranger-than-fiction mail-order-only antique business.

The one thing I like to brag about most is how in 1976 I bought and sold over 200,000 rare and semi-rare baseball gum and tobacco cards.

In all, I have attended over 7,500 auctions in my 50 years in this fun game, and my experiences would fill a larger book than this.

Of all the antiques I have bought and sold, I loved none more than Indian and oriental rugs. It is in my blood. Memories to most people are trips, baseball games, weddings. To me, they bring back all the 1,000 Indian rugs I once owned, which I can imagine lying under the desert sun with their bright reds, browns, grays and blues. Because of these rugs, I met all the greatest Indian rug and craft collectors in the nation, those who mailed thousands of dollars to me week after week to pay for rugs they'd never seen. These men and women, too, were a special breed. They would much rather wear rags than pass up a good Indian rug.

While antiques may lead a collector into becoming something less than a fashion plate, they do wonders in many cases to straighten up lost souls. Seeing lovely things all year round will make the village drunk or the village tough forget the booze and other blots on a man's good senses. In other words, antiquing has proved to be more fun than boozing or almost anything else. I hope you find it so.

Royal Bayreuth Sunbonnet
toothpick-holder
$250-$275

"The Little Sweeper,"
an action Kewpie, $350-$400

Googly-eyed doll made in Germany, AM No. 253, 9",
with watermelon smile, $850

Pincushion dolls, hands close to body, $25-$35; hands extended, $75 and up; complete original, $40-$50.

18″ Teddy with swivel arms and legs, signed Steiff, $400-$450; 1915 Raggedy Ann, if stamped on front torso "patented Sept. 7, 1915", $125-$150

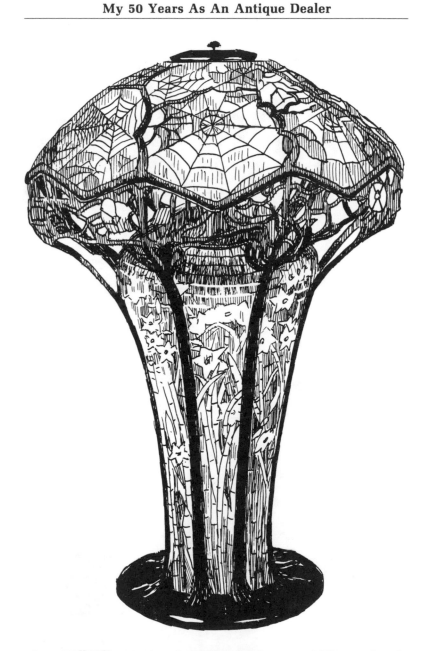

The 33″ tall Tiffany Spiderweb. Sold in 1980 for $360,000! From a photo by Christie's, New York.

36

WHY IS IT
ALL QUIET ON
THE AUCTION FRONT?

What's all the quiet about? There are at least 100 people on the sale grounds, but when I walk up, it becomes quiet. I'll tell you why. Until I appeared, there was hope in all hearts that this would be a field day, and a lot of antiques stolen with a cheap bid. Then all of a sudden, as blight disease affects growing crops, the happy looks are gone.

With my nation-wide contacts, I am a virtual encyclopedia of small and large orders aching to be filled. Therefore, not one oriental rug will escape my attention, nor a Mettlach stein, nor any of 2,900 different Royal Doulton figurines. If there is an Indian rug, it isn't going into the enemy's van, no matter if I lose on it, nor are any of 3,000 different cast iron banks. The biggies are not out of range of my guns, no matter if they include a signed Pairpoint, Handel or even Tiffany lamp. I will not let one good antique get by me. Now you can see what a professional can do to an auction.

The reason I do not intend to let even one good antique get away uncontested is because I cannot forget my first five or more years in the business when I was spreading my wings. It was a living hell I was put through by two or three dealers. I can still see Fred Knight, of Milledgeville, covering four or more sales at a time on Saturdays and Sundays, driving to Dixon to a sale with always three or four passengers in his station wagon and then jumping out with Jim, his 12-year-old prodigy, and walking fast through the sale making gestures to Jim, who with his pad and pencil was taking down the prices Fred would pay for everything good. Leaving Jim to bid for him, he would hurry to Polo, and one more rider, usually his mother, was left off there, and then on to Freeport, where he'd drop off his aunt. Then "The Knight" would high-tail it to the very best-sounding auction on that day that he had read of in the many newspapers he subscribed to. Thus Fred was bidding at four different sales, and not allowing me or anyone else to have even the leavings.

When Fred went into his bidding act, I would become an on-looker. He used to fire bids at the auctioneer so fast that the opposing bidders never knew what hit them. In this manner, Fred used to cure them forever of wanting to bid against him for even a toothpick, because he would either get an outright bargain, or he would let the opposing bidder have it so high he would have to hold it until ten years of inflation raised the price in order to break even on it.

I watched Fred for a few times go through his "stick 'em high" act, or practically steal an antique at an auction, and swore I was going to become another terror of the auction sales, both in the city and out on a manure pile 200 miles from nothing, and finally after 30 years I have succeeded in this unholy endeavor. I love to walk up to a crowd of antique bargain hunters, and seeing some rough opposition standing by a rarity, take the wind out of their sails by making an opening bid of half the antique's worth, such as $500 on a rare $1,000 beer stein. This is psychology, and if you can look as mean as I do when I bark out "Five hundred dollars," few will raise the bid. The other dealers will just walk away too shocked to say anything at the moment. They will say plenty around the supper table.

Once in a while, I will slacken up to let the collectors of depression glass and junk goofus glass and what I call minor collectibles have their prize without a bid from me. But I will bid on everything else--mink coats, diamonds, gold, coins, bronze statues, art glass, primitives, clothing, and all the rest, and I will either make money each time, or I will stick somebody so deep they will never pull the knife out.

So this is why it is all quiet as I approach a sale in any town within 75 miles of my home. But why do all the auctioneers break into broad smiles and holler hello? It's because they can rest assured that every antique on the sale bill is going to bring the biggest amount of money possible that day. This high bidding means a lot of money in their pockets at the rate of 20 to 25% of all items sold.

No one else speaks to me, as if death on horseback had just ridden up. The little things I do at auctions do not endear me to the bidders, and sometimes not even to the auctioneers. I love to pick up the rarest piece on a table and hold it up to the light, saying loud and clear that something is screwed up with it. I never say what I see wrong, just that it is "too bad." I rattle valuable glassware and dishes against one another to make it sound like they are being chipped or cracked.

Once at a sale back in the 60's a collector came up to me and said about a bank soon to be auctioned, "Dan, lay off that bank, will you? I collect them." To oblige him, I didn't bid. He bought the bank for $80 and didn't bother to say thank-you.

Later, Roy Stenzel told me, "Dan, that fellow doesn't collect banks, he sells banks." The "collector" had gotten a $600 bank away from me. Roy continued, "when you go to an auction, it's an auction. You don't have time to cater to everyone who comes up to you. This isn't a friendly game."

Since that time I have never asked a favor at a sale, nor have I given any to the scores of people who have come up to me and asked me to lay off this or that.

Today, after 50 years as a dealer, I've earned my stripes and deserve the fear that those stripes inspire. While fellow-bidders may not love me, the message I get through the tens of thousands of calls and letters I receive from out in Traderland is a different and better one.

Hatpins, circa 1900, $35-$75

37

ADDED TIPS ON HOW
TO MAKE EASY MONEY
WITHOUT EVEN HALF-WAY TRYING

Here is a review of items you may run across, with my tips on their value to you, garnered from my 50 years' experience as a dealer:

AFGHANS. Stay clear of this hand-work. It is one of the few hand-made articles that will be a loser for you if you pay very much for it.

ALADDIN LAMPS are sleepers that command some very high prices when made of colored glass. I just sold a lemon-colored Aladdin for $375. So keep your eyes open for unusual colors.

AMMUNITION BOXES. Paper ones of the 20's made by Winchester are very collectible and are always being advertised for.

ARCADE TOY COMPANY TOYS made in Free-port, Illinois, sell high. Look on the bottom of any old cast iron toy you find--Arcade many times has a hard-to-find signature. It could mean a profit of hundreds if you spot a signature that no one else does.

AUNT JEMINA ADS OR PRODUCT CON-TAINERS are one of the hundreds of Black collectibles that have been zooming in price every year since Martin Luther King was assassinated. Since Blacks can no longer be pictured in demeaning or humorous ways, memorabilia showing them so is one of today's green light investments. I mail music sheets picturing Blacks to New York for $10. An Amos 'n' Andy wind-up toy will bring $600.

BEADED BAGS will sell for $40 to $50, so buy all you can land for under $25.

JIM BEAM BOTTLES, AVON BOTTLES, and nearly all collector whiskey bottles are as dead for an investment as Christmas tree ornaments the day after. This goes for bottles made in the last 15 years. Antique bottles may still be a tremendous buy if you can find any.

BEER CANS. All old cone-top beer cans from the 20's and early 30's are a great investment. Any beer can with a cone top is worth a ten dollar bill, and many are in the $500 to $1,000 group. See *Antique Trader* ads.

BESWICK. These cute little figurines number around 50 different ones. Look for the name underneath. Most are selling for $20 to $40.

BONN. Royal Bonn china clocks are one of my very best selling clocks, and if you find one with outside escapement, you can usually sell it for $400 to $600. If it has just lots of roses and no outside escapement, a common 10 x 13″ clock sells for $350. Don't pass one up if under $300. Be on the look-out for a signature on the back.

Cone-top beer cans: Coronation, $50-$100; others, $40-$50. Pabst Blue Ribbon cone top brings $25-$35; Schlitz Vitamin D, $40-$50.

BOY AND GIRL SCOUT COLLECTIBLES. These are easy to find and command good prices. Watch the trade magazine classifieds for wanted pre-1940 Girl and Boy Scout objects.

CHICAGO 1893 WORLD'S FAIR and other fair items up to the 1933 World's Fair are sought after by fair collectors. The 1876 Philadelphia Fair, 1893 Chicago Fair, and 1904 St. Louis Fair mementoes are all good sellers.

COCA COLA. Pre-1916 Coca Cola ads found in magazines are very good and can be sold quickly to big Coke museums scattered around the country. Trays and signs up to 1940 sell well. Coca Cola collectibles are a big hobby spanning the nation. See trade paper ads for wanted items.

CLOTHING. Ladies' clothing of past eras is a surprise quick-sell today. I am referring to 1900's white underwear, with bloomers, petticoats, and chemises leading this clothing parade. The more lace the better. At nearly all Midwest sales where old people are transferred to nursing homes or are deceased, there will be a piece or two of white lace to be found and bought. Sometimes I have bought a cardboard box full, and then it is happy days, because it may kick out $400 worth of lacy underwear for quick shipment to some of the old clothes dealers who mostly sell to college kids. White pieces sell for $15 each, and the 20's flapper dresses for $30, while beaded ones go for $100 up. All long white cotton dresses are a sure thing for $75, and if especially fancy, $100 is assured.

COLLECTOR PLATES--at best a "comme ci comme ca" investment. I have seen a very poor demand during the past three years for collectors' plates. Nothing remains at high prices long that must stay

Designer dress, circa 1890's, $4,500; 1913 dress, $200.

stacked in a closet. This includes coins and sterling silver sets. Always buy the antiques and collectibles that can be easily displayed and seen. That is why we all buy antiques, isn't it?

DUCK DECOYS. Look for original paint in good condition. Buy only hollow decoys (recognizeable by the seam along the side). Even the saddest case of this type will sell for $40 to $50, and the better carvers' decoys are worth $1,000 to $5,000 each. Look to see if the feather painting is a work of art. Crow decoys sell for $600 when made by a well-known carver.

DENTAL EQUIPMENT if old finds a quick market with those who advertise in trade papers. Tools with black handles are circa 1900 and the highest priced. A small boxful may sell for $300 to an advertiser. Old dental chairs and cabinets are in big demand by dental museums.

DOILIES are worth $2 each. Good quality fancy work sells well. Crocheted tablecloths and bedspreads do not go begging. Buy such bedspreads for under $40 and tablecloths for under $15. Keep your eyes open for anything handmade today.

DRUGSTORE DISPLAY SIGNS and drugstore containers are almost as good as gold. Drugstore museums want all drugstore Americana at your price, and so do the country store hobbyists.

FISHING LURES of the 1920's and 30's, made of wood with glass eyes, bring about $10; $20 if the lure has six hooks. Some may go as high as $120, depending on the shape and the brand name of the lure.

JUICE EXTRACTORS or lemon reamers are one of the biggest sleepers. Those in colored glass may sell in three figures. There is a new reamer guidebook on the market that will open your eyes as to prices.

LIGHTNING RODS AND BALLS. Watch for balls in other shapes than round and in colors other than white and blue at farm sales.

MAJOLICA dishes are selling higher now all over the country than ever before. Buy all you can find for under $25 to $30 apiece.

MICROSCOPES of the 20's or earlier are good sellers, with black metal ones now selling for $100 and brass ones being sought after at $750 up.

MEDICAL INSTRUMENTS that you might find at a doctor's estate sale, if all steel, are worth around $500 for a small boxful of 25 or 30 instruments. Black handles are good, wooden handles better. Almost 100% of those who buy old doctors' instruments from me are themselves M.D.'s.

MUSICAL INSTRUMENTS are not a good buy at any price. Too many were made 50 years ago to ever become scarce and high priced. Banjos are the only exception.

NIPPON is one of the biggest collectible antiques in the country today. Because of the plentiful supply and because it is truly beautiful, keep your eyes open. Those with scenes in relief are best, the plaques or tobacco humidors with relief designs are worth $750 up. Dark blue is desirable, next comes scenics. Chocolate sets in Nippon are good sellers at $175.

PAPER GOODS are a must to know if you intend to go to the bank with your loot at least once in a while. Stay with all magazines earlier than 1930. Comic books before 1954 are winners, and **Playboy** is OK before 1960. Issue #1 of **Playboy** is fetching $500, with #2 a close second.

In comics, the #1 issue of **Superman**, printed in 1939, is worth $2,750; #1 1940 **Batman**, $2,000; #2

1940 **Whiz**, $4,500. These comics were once mass-produced. This means that sometime, somewhere, when you least expect it, one or a stack of these 1930-40 comics will be sold. Be ready to bid.

PENS that are made by Parker, W. E. Sheaffer, and 100 more companies during the 1910's and 20's are another big collectible today, with many selling for $1,000, such as the Parker Snake Pen that has a silver snake intertwined all down the pen barrel, and a pair of sterling silver snake's eyes at the end. I would advise you to stay with three or four major brands. Fat pens in mainline brands sell from $10 to $20 up. Try locating a Parker Snake Pen for a trip to Vegas.

POCKET KNIVES are a big money-maker if you can locate a Case XX knife or any of the better brands of the 20's and 30's such as Winchester, Remington, Ka-Bar, Parker, Shapleigh, and Keen Kutter. A Case XX pocket knife may sell from $200 to $500. Buy yourself a pocket knife price guide at your book store and study it.

STEREOPTICAN cards have increased in value five times since 1973, when a viewer and cards used to bring $30 to $35. Now all the young people are interested in them. Many cards, such as the stereo card tissues and scenes of the early West, are worth $5 to $10. Watch for cards showing Western town business districts in the 1870's and 80's and interiors of old stores and saloons. Indians sell high. The bigger, over-sized cards are the oldest and worth more. Look for buyers in trade magazines.

TEA LEAF IRONSTONE has emerged as my No. 1 best seller of all time in the ironstone field. Alfred Meakin Tealeaf is the most desirable. A cup and saucer will bring $75, while other pieces bring $50.

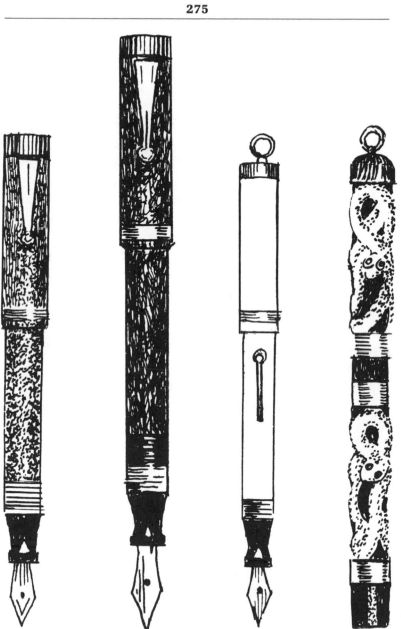

Parker pens circa 1927: large, around $100; medium, $35; lady's, $25. Snake pen, sterling value, about $1,000; gold-filled, $1,500.

Don't pay much for badly stained Tealeaf, and any piece with a chip or crack is not saleable at all. The reproduced Tealeaf of 10 years ago which almost killed the price of all Tealeaf is now very saleable, since the older type is hard to find. For the repro, pay 50% of the old Tealeaf current price.

TIN WIND-UP TOYS from the 30's to 50's such as Amos 'n' Andy, Charlie McCarthy, and Disney toys, sell for a minimum of $75, and may go up to $600. If you find a mint one in its original packing box, just go to a dealer and name your price.

SHIRLEY TEMPLE DOLLS are to me the surprise collectible of the entire doll industry. When Ideal first made them back in 1936, they were aimed for quick sale at low prices at Woolworth stores. They were sold in the millions. Buy any old Shirley Temple doll for under $150. In fair condition they will bring $200 and up. I sold a pair of 18″ 1936 Shirley Temple dolls in their packing boxes for $1,000.

Old blue depression glass with Shirley Temple picture and name sells for $25 to $60. Shirley Temple doll carriages are sold fast at $300 plus. Even though these items are all reproduced, it hasn't hurt old Shirl!

TOY IRONS are wanted by sad iron collectors. A child's iron in a swan shape sells quickly for $75. The ones with rope-shaped handles, so often found at sales, change hands for $40. All cast iron toy griddles find a new home for $60 to $75.

TAGS, DOG. 1920's and 30's and even later dog tags may be worth $5 to $10 to the hundreds of animal tag collectors who run ads in the trade papers. 1940's tags may bring $1 apiece, not bad if you find 100. If you should accidentally come across 100 or more pre-1900 dog tags, then be prepared to take a trip to

1930's 27" Shirley Temple with flirty eyes, $750-$800.

Las Vegas for a weekend, and then to the Gulf of Mexico for a week of marlin fishing, then to Monte Carlo to shoot dice and play roulette while horses' ovaries are passed to you on a silver tray. Next, to the French Riviera to swim next to the nudie beach on one side, with the girls from Africa sunning themselves on the other. When tired of using your binoculars, you can fly to the chalet you now own high in the Alps and watch all the skiers hit the slopes as you polish off hot buttered rum. In other words, keep a sharp look-out for pre-1900, beaten-up old dog tags, if only for this dream trip.

Old barber bottles, circa 1910, opalescent swirl, $65-$75; blue with enamel decor, $75-$85; milk glass, $40-$45. (Rarer art glass bottles, $150-$175.)

38

MY PREDICTIONS
FOR THE
ANTIQUE FUTURE

The antique industry has grown too fast over the past decade for its own good. There isn't anything old, of interest, that isn't called an antique or collector's item today. But articles that were made in the past 40 or 50 years cannot be classified with the fine antiques that were made before 1880 by our ancestors. The finer antiques were made even earlier, in the 1700's, and they are the ones that will always go up in price—never down. The only trouble with this kind of antique is its great scarcity, particularly west of the New England states. If all of us were to wait until a genuine piece of Sheraton, Hepplewhite, or Chippendale furniture showed up, we would be forced to stop collecting.

That is why, since 1972, all of us have taken to collecting almost anything made which is older and more plentiful.

I predict that these widely-made collector's items such as Depression glass will go down in price in the next few years rather than up, especially if depressed conditions should continue to put the squeeze on collecting. They may give a lot of pleasure in looking; but, at best, their price will stay the same. The finer antiques will continue to rise in price, because there is always the 10% of collectors who will not only sustain the prices of fine antiques with their buying power, but will continue to boost them higher as a blue ribbon investment.

For those with a lot of money to invest, quality oil paintings such as Remingtons and Russells, and 18th century American furniture are the best bets. For the rest of us, who do not have hundreds of thousands to spend, the best investments are early American handmade antiques such as quilts, dated coverlets, primitive paintings, rosemalled trunks and furniture, old samplers, and art pottery, plus Haviland china.

Oak furniture is also a good investment. It has become a top seller because young and old love to display it. Although walnut and oak furniture have run their course and will not continue to go up, I think they will stay up. An added advantage of furniture as a collectible is that it is not as easily stolen as coins or stamps. Also, I don't believe in investing money in things that have to be kept locked up in a vault and not enjoyed. Few are enjoying their coins or stamps these days.

Finally, buy quality, not quantity. Save your money until you can buy a quality piece. It will always be worth it when you sell. And look for one that is mint. Mint means someone cared enough to keep it that way for 75 to 100 years.

R.S. Prussia, "The Dice Throwers," $1,200-$1,400.

Two Important Tools For The
Astute Antique Dealer, Collector and Investor

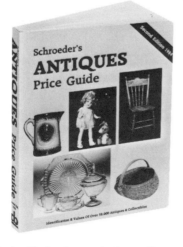

Schroeder's Antiques Price Guide

The very best low cost investment that you can make if you are really serious about antiques and collectibles is a good identification and price guide. We publish and highly recommend **Schroeder's Antiques Price Guide.** Our editors and writers are very careful to seek out and report accurate values each year. We do not simply change the values of the items each year but start anew to bring you an entirely new edition. If there are repeats, they are by chance and not by choice. Each huge edition (it weighs 3 pounds!) has over 56,000 descriptions and current values on 608 - 8½x11 pages. There are hundreds and hundreds of categories and even more illustrations. Each topic is introduced by an interesting discussion that is an education in itself. Again, no dealer, collector or investor can afford not to own this book. It is available from your favorite bookseller or antiques dealer at the low price of $9.95. If you are unable to find this price guide in your area, it's available from Collector Books, P. O. Box 3009, Paducah, KY 42001 at $9.95 plus $1.00 for postage and handling.

Schroeder's INSIDER and Price Update

A monthly newsletter published for the antiques and collectibles marketplace.

The **"INSIDER"**, as our subscribers have fondly dubbed it, is a monthly newsletter published for the antiques and collectibles marketplace. It gives the readers timely information as to trends, price changes, new finds, and market moves both upward and downward. Our writers are made up of a panel of well-known experts in the fields of Glass, Pottery, Dolls, Furniture, Jewelry, Country, Primitives, Oriental and a host of other fields in our huge industry. Our subscribers have that "inside edge" that makes them more profitable. Each month we explore 8-10 subjects that are "in", and close each discussion with a random sampling of current values that are recorded at press

time. Thousands of subscribers eagerly await each monthly issue of this timely 16-page newsletter. A sample copy is available for $3.00 postpaid. Subscriptions are postpaid at $24.00 for 12-months; 24 months for $45.00; 36 months for $65.00. A sturdy 3-ring binder to store your **Insider** is available for $5.00 postpaid. This newsletter contains NO paid advertising and is not available on your newsstand. It may be ordered by sending your check or money order to Collector Books, P. O. Box 3009, Paducah, KY 42001.